Understanding
history teaching

D0419749

Understanding history teaching

Chris Husbands, Alison Kitson and Anna Pendry

Open University Press
Maidenhead · Philadelphia

Open University Press
McGraw-Hill Education
McGraw-Hill House
Shoppenhangers Road
Maidenhead
Berkshire
England
SL6 2QL

email: enquiries@openup.co.uk
world wide web: www.openup.co.uk.

and

325 Chestnut Street
Philadelphia, PA 19106, USA

First Published 2003

A catalogue record of this book is available from the British Library

ISBN 0 335 21271 9 (pb)   0 335 21272 7 (hb)

Library of Congress Cataloging-in-Publication Data
CIP data applied for

Typeset by RefineCatch Limited, Bungay, Suffolk
Printed in Great Britain by Biddles Limited, *www.biddles.co.uk*

For Martin Roberts

Contents

List of tables and figures

Tables

Figures

Preface

This book explores the nature of history teaching at a time of rapid and profound change in the study of history, in the organization and management of the school curriculum and in education generally. We try to explore the ways in which history teachers work in classrooms and the different sorts of expertise on which they draw. In doing so, we hope that we contribute to the developing – and contested – knowledge base on which researchers can draw, but equally we hope that our work itself contributes to dialogue between history teachers about the sources and nature of their effectiveness. We have therefore tried to write for both academic and professional audiences and we hope that our methods, our findings and our conclusions will be of interest to both.

The book is organized in three sections, each containing three chapters. The first section, Understanding history education, introduces underlying themes in history education research and practice, as well as introducing the case study schools which form the basis for our analysis. In this section, we set the book in the context of recent professional practice in history education and of research in and beyond history teaching. The second section, Understanding history teachers, is firmly rooted in history classrooms: we analyse history lessons and explore the nature and range of the knowledge which history teachers deploy. In Chapter 4, the focus is on individual teachers, beginning with descriptive analyses of single lessons; in Chapters 5 and 6 we move from individual lessons and teachers to general accounts of teacher knowledge and practice. The final section, Understanding the history curriculum, broadens the focus from classrooms to history curricula. We consider the ways in which curricula in schools are constructed and the purposes they are designed to serve, before drawing together the analysis and themes of the book in the final chapter. Each chapter in the book is organized around an over-arching question; the questions themselves are designed to stimulate reflection on the themes of the book.

The book is written to understand history teaching, but also, we hope, to develop it. It is useful to set out in a little more detail what we mean by understanding and developing history teaching. This is not a book which sets out to prescribe ways of teaching. Instead, it tries to describe in some detail the practices and strategies of experienced history teachers as a way of understanding in more detail why they work in the ways that they do. We see a clear and detailed understanding of history teachers' practice as an essential basis for attempting to develop the ways in which history teachers work: not by offering prescriptions about 'good' or 'effective' practice, but by building out from the ways teachers already work. Too often prescriptions for improvement and policies for change have been developed on the basis of partial, incomplete or negative accounts of what teachers do or do not do. In this book, we offer an analysis of the richness and sophistication of history teachers' work which we hope provides a more secure starting point for moving the discipline forward.

The book was researched between 1999 and 2001 and completed during the academic year 2001–2002. At a time of rapid – indeed accelerating – change in the secondary curriculum, this time-scale presented inevitable difficulties for writing up, and we have tried to explore the ways in which developments after the research was conducted might impinge on our data. The fieldwork was completed by all three authors, with Chris Husbands working in two schools, Alison Kitson in two and Anna Pendry in four. In terms of writing, Section 1 was initially drafted by Chris Husbands, Section 2 by Anna Pendry and Section 3 by Alison Kitson, but drafts were swapped and re-written extensively – one of the great advantages of writing collaborative books in an age of electronic mail! Again, Anna's contribution to the final text is more extensive than that of Alison or Chris.

Inevitably, we have accumulated a variety of debts in writing the book. We are deeply indebted to the Nuffield Foundation, whose generosity funded the research at the centre of the book between 1999 and 2001. We are equally indebted to the history teachers and departments with whom this research funding enabled us to work. The protocols of research anonymity prevent us from acknowledging their contribution to this book publicly, but we are grateful and were humbled by their generosity with their time, expertise and knowledge. A further debt is to the work of Martin Booth, whose ground-breaking 1969 study *History Betrayed?* is in many ways the intellectual starting point for our work. Booth unlocked the ways in which history teaching operated in the late 1960s and in many ways paved the way for the generation of reform and development which has reshaped the discipline in schools. While we question many of Booth's conclusions, neither this book nor the practices we describe would have been the same without his work. We have also accumulated intellectual debts to our colleagues at Oxford and Warwick and in the history education community more generally who have commented on different aspects of the book or who have offered advice on different aspects. In particular, we should like to thank Liz Bills, Katharine Burn, Christine Counsell, Deb Cunningham, Terry Haydn, Peter Lee and Daniel Muijs for their comments, both on elements of the text and the issues it addresses. We know that they will not necessarily agree with all that we say, but our gratitude to them is no less. Louisa Hopkins provided outstanding secretarial and research support at various stages of the book and we are grateful to her for her unstinting and professional work.

The book is dedicated to Martin Roberts, who over 40 years has been an inspirational history teacher, thinker about the history curriculum and headteacher. In different ways, we have all three been privileged to work with him and to learn from him – the book is a modest expression of our thanks.

Chris Husbands, Alison Kitson and Anna Pendry

SECTION 1
Understanding history education

1 What's happening in history teaching?

From cloudless skies: the world of history and the dilemmas of professional practice

On 11 September 2001 four American Airlines planes were hijacked with the intention of using them as missiles. Two were flown into each of the twin towers of the World Trade Center in New York some 20 minutes apart, one onto the Pentagon building and one, possibly intended for the White House, crashed into countryside in Pennsylvania. Visual images of the attack on the World Trade Center dominated news coverage within minutes. The immediate impact of the images flashed around the world was devastating; there was an immediate sense of an event of enormous political, diplomatic, strategic and historical significance. Television screens endlessly repeated the image of the second aeroplane crashing into the second of the World Trade Center towers, but the dominance of the terrifying image was accompanied by wild speculation built on a paucity of hard information. What had happened, why it had happened, what its intended impact was and what its consequences might be – all these were unclear. By the next day, connections were already being made between American foreign policy, the Al-Qaeda network and the complex politics of the Middle East, but information and detail were, of course, still frustratingly scarce. The images – unforgettable images of aeroplanes moving across the cloudless sky, then being deployed as missiles and carefully piloted to make an impact at just the right point to ensure the collapse of the building; of smoke rising in a clear plume from one of the world's tallest buildings; of humans, tiny specks on television screens, seeking to escape from the buildings by suicidally jumping from upper storeys; of the towers collapsing in on themselves into vast clouds of dust – had already been projected into the consciousness of adults and young people across the globe (Prins 2002). On 12 September, questions abounded which would be more or less conclusively answered in the days and months which followed, although all posed underlying questions which will remain unresolved for many years

(Halliday 2002). Who was responsible for what was clearly a spectacularly orchestrated act of terrorism? How had it been possible to coordinate the hijackings? What beliefs and ideologies underpinned the actions of those responsible? What – in the febrile atmosphere created by saturation coverage in the press, on the television, on the Internet – might happen next? What would be the reaction of the American government? What consequences would flow from the appalling incident – for America, for the Middle East, for the wider world?

These were political questions and media questions, but they were also questions for history teachers in the immediate aftermath of the attacks of 11 September. History teachers faced unanticipated professional dilemmas. How should they teach in the days following 11 September? How far should their planned, prescribed curricula be abandoned? For them, and for the young people they taught, there were obvious immediate (though still historical) questions: how would this incident change the world into which they were growing and how might it impact on their own lives? In the atmosphere of confusion and ignorance prevalent on 12 September, they were questions tinged with real fear: would there be other attacks? Would there be immediate retaliation? What would such retaliation unleash? If passenger aeroplanes could be used as weapons of mass destruction, what other perversions of everyday life might be anticipated? Adolescents at school on 12 September were traumatized by the endlessly repeated images, confused by the events, but also very frightened. Unanticipated, unexpected, unplanned, the terrorist attacks posed questions and challenges for all teachers, but perhaps particularly for history teachers: these were questions which reach to the heart of the discipline of history as a school subject. September 11, especially in immediate perspective, was an event of world historical significance.

History teachers deal, of course, with events of compelling significance: the sack of Rome in AD 476, the fall of Constantinople a thousand years later, the French Revolution of 1789, the dropping of the atomic bomb on Hiroshima in 1945. They typically try to explain these events for young people, enabling them to relate the events to a framework of explanation which unpacks the past in terms of young people's conceptions of the world. Where did 11 September 2001 fit against, say, 14 July 1789, or 4 August 1914, or 3 September 1939, or 6 August 1945? What sort of event was it (Prins 2002)? What was its significance (Hunt 2000: 39–53)? What could they do, or say, on 12 September? What connections could be made between what was already known and what everyone wanted to know?

The professional dilemmas were acute: given an event of apparently cataclysmic significance, which spoke powerfully from the depths of modern history, to which all their pupils had, so to speak, already been vicarious witnesses, how might history teachers approach their lessons on 12 September? These dilemmas were multi-faceted: was it professionally sensible to address the issues directly at all or, which is similar, was it professionally defensible not to address the issue? In what circumstances might it be professionally defensible to ignore, in 12 September's history lessons, what had happened on 11 September? How far might the necessity of responding to the events of 11 September be outweighed by a reluctance to deal with situations where so many of the facts were as yet unknown, or a desire to protect young people from damaging exposure to an already traumatic set of images and events, or the pressing need to maintain pupils' focus on work in progress? Some teachers recalled their own experience as pupils during the Cuban missile crisis, when the widespread perception that nuclear war was imminent made it apparently pointless for their teachers to deliver the planned curriculum. Already, decisions about whether and how to respond were being set against the refracting lens of professional expertise, which identifies the urgent and the pressing and provides some sort of spectrum against which innovation and development might be set. Beyond this, the professional dilemmas were refracted through enormously significant contextual professional judgements. How might the decisions on whether, and how, to address the issues be affected by the teacher's judgements about the emotional, intellectual and affective maturity of their pupils? How might the events of 11 September be addressed with a mixed attainment class of 12-year-olds, as opposed, say, to a high-attaining and well-read class of 17-year-olds? How might the decisions on whether and how to address the issues be affected by the location of the school and the ethnic and religious composition of classes? Under-reported on 12 September, in some British cities – just as in the townships of the West Bank – minorities in Islamic populations had reacted to what appeared to be a humbling of America by celebrating the events of 11 September with flag burning and singing. In weeks to come, teachers, and especially those in schools with substantial Islamic populations, would need to develop strategies which would address popular Islamophobia: again, the professional judgements about what to teach and how to teach it were mediated by teachers' implicit understandings of the contexts in which they teach and the materials with which they work. The events of 11 September were addressed in a multitude of ways on 12 September in history classrooms. Rarely, if at all, ignored, they were explored in different ways, using different media, in classrooms by teachers drawing on their own professional resources and expertise to mediate their understanding of the events and their understanding of the needs, interests and assumptions of their pupils.

This book explores the ways in which history teachers deploy their professional expertise, their understanding of the nature of history as an academic and school subject, and their understanding of their pupils, to generate a variety of cognitive and affective outcomes from the learning and study of history in schools. It follows other researchers in arguing that 'teaching involves the incessant making of decisions' (Bage 2001: 24; see also

Calderhead 1984). The professional dilemmas of 11 September threw into sharp relief the everyday dilemmas which underlie the teaching and learning of history. If we live in an increasingly unsettled world, and one further destabilized by the events of 11 September, then we teach children who are growing into an increasingly uncertain future. This too provided a dimension for the handling of the events of 11 September in the classroom. For a generation and a half after the end of the Second World War, history teachers had developed well-grounded strategies and curricula which addressed the themes of superpower rivalry, European integration and the development of traditions of tolerance and democracy. The 1990s, the decade of Srebrenica, of the Rwandan genocide, of the collapse of the Soviet Union, undermined many of the established assumptions about the content of post-war school history. The opening of the twenty-first century appeared to raise further questions about how relationships between past and present, and between different perspectives, might be handled in the classroom. At a time of rapid and complex change, 'History is an often unsettling and sometimes uncomfortable subject. It is controversial and often very sensitive. There is some consensus about its importance in the school curriculum but much less agreement about what it is for' (Slater 1995: xi).

This book examines the ways in which history teachers have themselves, in their day-to-day work with pupils and with colleagues, worked out 'what it is for', by examining the ways in which history curricula are developed and deployed and by examining the relationship between what history teachers in their professional lives do and what they aspire to achieve. It explores in the light of a detailed study of classrooms and school history curricula and in the light of wider research, the nature of history teachers' professional expertise and seeks to understand and explain this expertise in the context of their work in classrooms with pupils. It advances a series of arguments about the nature of history teaching. The first central argument of the book is to place the history teacher at the centre of thinking about teaching in history classrooms. This seems something of a truism. However, too often curriculum reform and research conceptualize teachers passively. They 'implement' reform, they 'respond' to debate, they 'experience' professional development. Our argument is different. We argue that teachers make curricula and shape learning based on a complex interrelationship between their assumptions about the discipline, their response to pupil needs and their short- and long-term aims. History teachers responded differently on 12 September to the events of 11 September. We offer some explanations for different practice based on the active engagement of teachers with their professional practice. Our second central argument is a consequence of this. We argue that in order to unlock reform and development, it is essential to understand not only teacher practice but also teacher thinking. By looking closely at the way teachers work in classrooms, we unlock a richer picture of professional practice than has hitherto been available. Our third argument is to stress the interrelationship of classroom practice and the aims and purposes of teaching, articulated through a single secondary school subject. We aim to draw together a series of lenses on professional practice, and thus to inform both thinking and the development of practice. We begin, in this chapter, by exploring the professional and practical world of history education over the last 35 years.

Shaping history in schools: two traditions

History teachers are – as we shall see – diverse in many ways. They differ in obvious ways: age, gender, ethnicity, cultural background, intellectual training and, beneath these obvious differences, they have different conceptions of what school history is for, how and why it should be taught and what sort of intellectual and educational pursuit it is. But nearly all history teachers will agree that history is a peculiarly complex subject to teach, and to learn. All subjects are difficult to teach, but the particular difficulties of teaching history derive from the relationship between the history teacher, pupils and the past. History teaching deals, by definition, with things which are neither immediate nor present, whether they are the funerary practices of the Anglo-Saxons, the social structure of the medieval village, the belief systems of early modern witch hunters, the ideological underpinnings of the French Revolution or the political consequences of the Treaty of Versailles (Husbands 1996). While most arguments for the place of history in the school curriculum include some notion that an understanding of the present and the immediate demands an understanding of the past, effective history teaching frequently does this by making the present less familiar and immediate, grounding it in a grasp of historical detail and origin. Its raw materials and underpinning concepts are frequently complex in structure, language and focus. Even superficially familiar words might involve shifting, subject-specific meanings (Edwards 1978; Husbands 1996). The sequential, narrative structure of the past provides an essential, though ultimately insufficient frame of reference for understanding the underlying ideas of the subject (Rogers 1978; Bage 1999). The outcomes of learning history are frequently described in the most illusory of terms: at the highest levels the understanding of history is an understanding of complexity, uncertainty and the limits of knowledge (Lee and Ashby 1987; Shemilt 1987). The fictional history teacher in Graham Swift's haunting novel, *Waterland*, asks, 'What is a History teacher?' and then develops an answer,

> he's someone who teaches mistakes. While others say, Here's how to do it, he says, And here's what goes wrong. While others tell you, This is the way, this is the path, he says, And here are a few bungles, botches, blunders and fiascoes . . . It doesn't work out; it's human to

> err . . . He's an obstructive instructor, treacherous tutor. Maybe he's
> a bad influence. Maybe he's not good to have around.
>
> (Swift 1983: 183)

These complexities have given rise to a series of competing accounts of the
nature and purposes of the subject in schools and, perhaps in consequence, a
rather uncertain status for the subject in the school curriculum (Phillips 1998).
For explanatory purposes we distinguish two traditions of history teaching,
one, tellingly described by Sylvester (1994) as the 'great tradition' and another,
rather more amorphous, learner centred alternative tradition; each tradition
encompasses a range of possible classroom and intellectual approaches to the
study of the past, and there may be frequent borrowing and cross-fertilization
between the traditions. Nonetheless, to distinguish the two traditions points
up some sharp divergences in the teaching of the subject. In the United
Kingdom, history teaching was, *par excellence*, a central component of the
curriculum which emerged from public and grammar schools in the nine-
teenth and twentieth centuries (Chancellor 1970). For the majority of
the twentieth century, history teaching in schools, and particularly in the
grammar schools, was dominated by the 'great tradition'. In this 'great tradition' the history teacher's role was 'didactically active'; it was to give pupils
the facts of historical knowledge and to ensure through repeated short tests
that they had learned them. The pupil's role was passive; history was a
'received subject'. The body of knowledge to be taught was also clearly defined.
It was 'mainly British political history, with some European, from Julius Caesar
to 1914' (Sylvester 1994: 9). In somewhat different terms, John Slater teased
readers about the underlying assumptions of the knowledge base of this 'great
tradition',

> content was largely British, or rather Southern English; Celts looked
> in to starve, emigrate, or rebel; the North to invent looms or work in
> mills; abroad was of interest once it was part of the Empire; foreigners
> were either, sensibly, allies, or, rightly, defeated.
>
> (Slater 1989: 1)

The 'great tradition' defined the terms in which pupils in schools
encountered the past and it did so, as Sylvester's account demonstrates, by
making three interlocking assumptions about pedagogy, content and
purposes. In terms of *pedagogy*, the 'great tradition' prescribed, as we have seen,
a didactically active role for the teacher, placing high premium on the
teacher's ability to construct active interpretations of history and a generally
passive role for the learner, who was required to assimilate, organize and
either reproduce or, exceptionally, reinterpret the teacher's interpretation. The
pedagogic expertise of the history teacher thus resided in his or her command

of, and ability to relate, subject matter knowledge. In terms of *content*, as we have seen, the 'great tradition' placed emphasis on the primacy of political English history, and, by extension, imperial history. Content, in the 'great tradition' was largely organized chronologically, moving from the Roman invasion of AD 43 through to the twentieth century and using the frame of high politics to sequence and structure knowledge about the past (Booth 1969; Chancellor 1970; Sylvester 1994). Finally, the 'great tradition' made assumptions about the *purposes* of history teaching. History was taught for largely intrinsic and cultural reasons (Slater 1995); at its heart lay the acquisition of relatively complex knowledge about an assumed shared national political culture and there were strong connections between the nature of the school history syllabus and the Whig interpretation of a largely progressive development of democracy, welfare and improvement. Curriculum guidelines and research findings throughout the twentieth century attest to the enormous influence of the 'great tradition' on practice and theory. There have been relatively few empirically grounded studies of the teaching and learning of history, but Martin Booth offered a detailed analysis of the school history curriculum in four schools in the 1960s, where the 'great tradition' reigned supreme (Booth 1969).

More recently, the influence of the 'great tradition' reached into the construction of the national curriculum, introduced in English schools in 1991. In his supplementary guidance to the working group established to advise the Secretary of State for Education on the content of the history curriculum, Kenneth Baker insisted that school history should 'help pupils come to understand how a free and democratic society has developed over the centuries', placing at its 'core the history of Britain, the record of its past and, in particular its political, constitutional and cultural heritage' (DES 1990). In 1998, the Qualifications and Curriculum Authority (QCA), the government body charged with overseeing the review of the national curriculum, indicated that 'the school curriculum should contribute to the development of pupils' sense of identity through knowledge and understanding of their . . . social and cultural heritages . . . It should pass on the enduring values of society' (QCA 1998: 5).

The assumptions underpinning the 'great tradition' have never been uncontested. Indeed, Richard Aldrich has demonstrated that the primacy of this 'great tradition' was challenged from the moment of its inception in the wake of the 1902 Education Act which extended central control over the elementary curriculum. As early as 1910, M.W. Keatinge outlined a rationale and method for the use of historical evidence in the classroom (Keatinge 1910). But the assumptions did not come under sustained pressure until the ferment of curriculum development unleashed following the establishment of the Schools' Council in 1963. The Schools' Council established projects which asked fundamental questions about the organization and structure of the curriculum in England and Wales. Under Piagetian influence, Schools' Council projects questioned the assumptions about pedagogy and teaching which underpinned the 'great tradition'. The most significant were: the Schools' Council History (13–16) Project (SHP), established by the Schools' Council at the University of Leeds from 1972 to 1976 under the leadership of David Sylvester; the Humanities Curriculum Project (HCP) established from 1968 to 1974 at the University of East Anglia under the direction of Lawrence Stenhouse; and the Schools' Council Place, Time and Society (8–14) project established at the London University Institute of Education from 1971 to 1975 (Blyth 1975; Stenhouse 1975). Cumulatively, the Schools' Council projects of the late 1960s spawned an alternative tradition of history teaching with quite different assumptions about the role of the teacher, the organization and selection of content and the purposes of the subject.

Where the 'great tradition' placed teacher expertise at the centre of its pedagogy, the SHP and the Schools' Council Place, Time and Society project placed the learner's role in developing knowledge at the centre. Stenhouse outlined a radical pedagogy for HCP, in which the teacher was to be construed as a 'neutral chair', introducing learners to sources of information and supporting them, thorough discussion, in reaching an understanding of the problems under investigation (Stenhouse 1968). In SHP Sylvester and his colleagues shifted attention to the skills learners needed to make sense of historical problems – skills in understanding evidence, in comparing divergent accounts and reaching their own conclusion (Schools' Council 1976).

At the same time, the appropriate content of the history curriculum was radically questioned. Here, the development of history teaching crosscut with the development of the historical discipline. Historians such as E.P. Thompson, whose radical history of the making of the English working class sought to rescue the poor from 'the enormous condescension of posterity' (Thompson 1965: 13), Sheila Rowbotham, who demonstrated the histories of women 'hidden from history' (Rowbotham 1973) and Eric Hobsbawm whose studies explored the cultures of bandits on the margins of European and colonial societies (Hobsbawm 1969) were hugely influential. Innovative methodologies, an interest in the experiences of the dispossessed and oppressed and a new openness to influences from sociology and anthropology transformed the concerns of academic history, and thus the academic training of history graduates (Samuel 1994; Burke 2001). The content base of history degrees shifted markedly in the 1960s and 1970s, with consequent implications for the knowledge and conceptual base of those graduates who subsequently became teachers. School textbooks, under the influence of the reprographics revolution, lost their dominance and, at a time of curriculum innovation, pupils in classrooms found themselves exploring the history of the native Americans, of peoples in Peru and the Arctic. Assumptions about content were shifting in far from radical quarters over the decade and a half following 1970 and in 1985, in an influential discussion of *History in the Primary and Secondary Years*, Her Majesty's Inspector (HMI) asserted that 'No history teacher can duck the question "In what way should the history syllabus in this school be different because my pupils live in a multicultural society?" ' (HMI 1985: 30).

Finally, the alternative tradition asked questions about the purposes of generating knowledge in history and humanities classrooms. Where the 'great tradition' frequently took the purposes of history teaching in schools for granted, exponents of the alternative tradition were more critical. A variety of curriculum development projects explored different justifications for the place of history or the humanities in the school curriculum. In some curriculum development projects, subjects were regarded as what Alan Blyth in the Place, Time and Society project called 'resources', which offered different components of pedagogy or style to a curriculum (Blyth 1975). For Lawrence Stenhouse who was critical of a subject-based curriculum, the focus should properly be on issues rather than subjects, and issues about which society had failed to give a wholly consensual or clear answer. In the Humanities Curriculum Project, the emphasis was on the deployment of historical insights and skills alongside others in discussion: given divisions in society over issues of controversy, teachers' obligations were to teach the dispute and the reasons for it, rather than a point of view within the dispute. For Stenhouse, the critical contribution of history to debate and discussion was its appeal to evidence (Labbett 1996). The most thorough-going attempt to address the issue of the purposes of history teaching in schools was attempted in the Schools' Council History Project. In frequent misrepresentation, the project is seen as attempting to provide a curriculum justification of school history around a set of historical 'skills' in analysing, comparing and evaluating disparate evidence in order to construct a historical account. In fact the project began from a quite different perspective, as an attempt to think through a justification for history in terms of the needs of adolescents at a time of rapid change and in the face of widespread predictions that the young people of the 1970s would experience hugely increased leisure time. The project then developed a curriculum specification for history (Labbett 1979) which addressed both content and ways of working. Crucially, however, it established that the justification for the place of history in the school curriculum had to be couched conceptually both in terms of the discipline and in terms of what the discipline contributed to learners and their curriculum. There were two important consequences. The first was seen in the long-term influence of the project on national- and school-level objectives for the teaching of history, whether in early formulations of specifications for the outcomes of history (Coltham and Fines 1970) or in the series of subject specifications for history in public examinations. The second was somewhat more paradoxical. The elaboration of curriculum specifications for history in terms of learners' wider general education provided history teachers with a set of intellectual resources with which to engage with the development of vocational education a decade later. By articulating a coherent rationale for history education in terms of the wider curriculum, the project gave it an intellectual basis with which to thrive in the face of attempts to restructure the secondary curriculum around skills-led initiatives.

The national curriculum and its development

By the time of the introduction of the national curriculum the 'great tradition' was under substantial attack from a quite different tradition of history teaching. Across English schools, history teachers and their departments took up often radically different positions on the assumptions of the two competing traditions (Barker 2002). The conflict between these traditions, worked out in pamphlets, local education authority (LEA) curriculum guidance and media outlets, has been outstandingly described by Rob Phillips (1998).

Table 1.1 The two traditions of history teaching

	The 'great tradition'	The alternative tradition
Learners and pedagogy	• Emphasizes the didactically active role of the teacher. • Assumes a high level of teacher subject knowledge. • Learner's role is largely passive.	• Emphasizes constructivist models of learner engagement with the past. • Places a premium on teacher's ability to manage student learning activities.
Content	• Characterized by a concern with national history. • Focuses on the understanding of the present through engagement with the past.	• Characterized by a variety of content reflecting world history and the experiences of a variety of groups. • Stresses the importance of learning about a variety of historical situations and contexts.
Purposes of learning history	• Defined through the content of the subject. • Focuses substantially on the cultural capital of historical content.	• Defined through the contribution of the subject to wider general education. • Focuses substantially on preparation for working life and the acquisition of skills.

The traditions defined the intellectual landscape of history education in the last two decades of the twentieth century and, as a result, sharpened professional dilemmas about content, pedagogy and outcomes. More than this, the traditions co-existed in different ways in different schools, departments and individual teachers. There were those firmly embedded at one extreme or another of each tradition, but most history teachers moved, in terms of their own practice, between the different assumptions of the two traditions. This was possible because of the structure of the first national curriculum, which was published in 1990 and implemented from September 1991, and based around a policy compromise which appeared to hold the two traditions in creative tension. *Content* was specified in considerable detail through a sequence of programmes of study, themselves to be arranged chronologically through each key stage, with a common core of British history and optional units requiring study of European and world history. On the other hand, historical *skills* and *concepts* were specified by three attainment targets which defined the basis on which the content was to be organized: Attainment Target 1 was defined as 'Knowledge and understanding of history', Attainment Target 2 as 'Interpretations of history' and Attainment Target 3 as 'The use of historical sources' (Table 1.2). Content, skills and concepts were brought together in the assessment level descriptors which defined expected outcomes for learners at each of ten levels of attainment. An understandable response

Table 1.2   Attainment targets (1991) and key elements (1995, 2000) in the history national curriculum

1991 National curriculum		*1995/2000 National curriculum knowledge, skills and understanding*	
Attainment target 1	Knowledge and understanding of history	Key element 1	Chronological understanding
Attainment target 2	Interpretations of history	Key element 2	Knowledge and understanding of events, people and changes in the past
Attainment target 3	The use of historical sources	Key element 3	Historical interpretation
		Key element 4	Historical enquiry
		Key element 5	Organization and communication

Source: QCA (2000)

to the introduction of the national curriculum from 1991 was an attempt to develop teaching strategies which delivered the detail of the prescription of the 1991 specifications in both content and in skills-led outcomes, in other words to draw on both traditions while focusing lesson planning and activities around the intended outcomes in the level descriptors. In some schools there were attempts both to address the content prescriptions of the national curriculum and to develop skills with concomitant overload on both students and teachers.

In 1995, the national curriculum was substantially revised. Prescription of content was trimmed, the level of prescription reduced, the number of attainment targets reduced from three to one, and the number of levels of attainment was reduced from ten to eight. Five key elements (Table 1.2) sought to clarify the underlying ideas of history in schools, encouraging teachers to teach in a more holistic fashion, which developed historically specific and communication skills through sequences of historical content. Redesignating Attainment Target 3 ('The use of historical sources') as 'historical enquiry', Key Element 4 was particularly helpful in encouraging teachers to think in enquiry-led ways where pupils might use evidence to construct tentative answers to historical questions. This contrasts with the approach to source work often taken in the early years of the national curriculum, succinctly described as 'death by sources A to F' (Counsell 2000a). The continued presence of historical interpretations (now knowledge, skills and understanding) since 1991 ensures that a proper aim of history teaching is for pupils to develop an understanding of the nature of history as a study and interpretation of the past. There is therefore strong professional evidence that the practice of history teaching has moved beyond both the 'great' and the alternative traditions in important ways. This is particularly the case in relation to pedagogy and content. Here, much current practice appears to have resolved debates between what Christine Counsell has called 'the distracting dichotomy' of skills and content (Counsell 2000b). What is less clear is the extent to which current practice has resolved the tensions between competing ideas about the purposes of history teaching. As we shall see, there are explanations for this in terms of the new pressures on history in the school curriculum. The most recent revision of the national curriculum has removed further prescription, enabling teachers to plan creatively and flexibly, while retaining the key elements – in knowledge, skills and understanding – with only very minor changes. We need to explore the extent to which teachers have exploited the flexibility of the 2000 national curriculum and the ways in which they have drawn on the different traditions of history teaching in doing so.

Professional challenges and professional practice

In this section we explore the current position of history in the school curriculum and consider some of the policy and professional issues which impinge on history teachers' work. In particular, we explore four issues which in different ways pose challenges to the way history is planned, organized and taught in secondary schools: the position of history in the school curriculum, the development of citizenship education, the implementation of the national Key Stage 3 Strategy and the changing organization and structure of secondary schooling.

Throughout the post-war period the position of history in schools was uncertain: strong in the early years of the secondary school, it was an optional subject for pupils aged between 14 and 16 and optional again for pupils studying A level. In some primary schools history was strong, but research and inspection evidence suggested that such schools were relatively rare. The 1988 Education Reform Act, by establishing history as a foundation subject in the national curriculum for pupils aged between 5 and 16, appeared to transform the subject in the school curriculum. In practice, a series of policy reviews and a reshaping of the curriculum subsequently weakened this position. From 1991, history ceased to be compulsory for 14–16-year-olds. In 1998, the requirement on primary schools to teach the full national curriculum was eased as part of the government's focus on primary literacy and numeracy. In 2002 history remains a compulsory element of the curriculum for pupils in English schools aged 5–14, but is an optional element of the curriculum for 14–16-year-olds and for those who decide to continue academic study beyond the age of 16. Recent moves to allow schools to experiment with novel structures for 14–19-year-olds, and to lay the foundations for these structures at ages 11–14 raise further questions about the security of the discipline in schools (Husbands 2001). In many respects then, the formal and practical position of history remains similar to that which was obtained in the early 1970s: a strong presence in the curriculum for 11–14-year-olds, an optional presence in the curriculum for 14–19-year-olds, and a limited presence in the primary curriculum. There is stronger quantitative evidence to suggest that history now occupies a precarious position in many schools (Husbands 2001). The main basis for this claim lies in data on patterns of entries for public examinations, and particularly for GCSE examinations. GCSE examination statistics allow us to trace the number of students entered for all examinations at age 16 and the number and proportion of these entered for history. The data for the period 1989–2002 are presented in Figure 1.1. While GCSE entries as a whole rose by almost 10 per cent over the 13 years following the 1988 Education Reform Act – and especially in the mid-1990s – the number of entries for GCSE history fell over the period as a whole. Entries were falling in

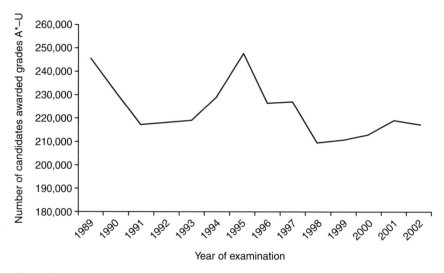

Figure 1.1   History GCSE entries, 1989–2002

the late 1980s and early 1990s, before rising sharply in 1994 and 1995 as part of the general increase in examination entries. In 1992, the government began to publish examination league tables and schools increased examination entries largely as a result. But 1995 was GCSE history's high point – entries fell by over 15 per cent between 1996 and 1998. In spite of a modest recovery in overall numbers of history examination entries thereafter, the increase was smaller than the overall increase in GCSE entries as schools continued to expand examination activity and as school populations rose. By 2002 history was markedly weaker in the school curriculum than it had been in 1989: there were 10 per cent fewer entries than there had been in 1989, and history accounted for a smaller proportion of all GCSE entries than it had in 1989, the proportion having fallen each year since 1995 (Table 1.3 and Figure 1.1). One of the key issues for this study is the ways in which history departments are responding to these developments.

While history's position in the school curriculum was weakening through the 1990s, new challenges to the place of the subject in the secondary curriculum developed. Two are of particular importance: the development of citizenship education after the 1997 election and the implementation of the national Key Stage 3 Strategy after 2001. Citizenship had been highlighted as a cross-curricular theme following the 1988 Education Reform Act, and immediately following the implementation of the subject-based national curriculum there were a series of publications, including one from the House of Commons Speaker's Commission on Citizenship, which explored the scope, content, pedagogy and practice of education for citizenship education

Table 1.3 GCSE grades A*–U awarded 1993–2002: all subjects and history

Year	All subjects	% change	History	% change	% all entries
1989	5,132,988		244,452		4.76
1990	5,016,547	−2.27	229,660	−6.05	4.58
1991	4,947,593	−1.37	217,020	−5.50	4.39
1992	5,025,548	1.64	218,279	0.58	4.34
1993	4,968,634	−1.19	219,192	0.42	4.41
1994	5,029,599	1.23	229,466	4.69	4.56
1995	5,431,625	7.99	247,929	8.05	4.56
1996	5,475,872	0.81	226,808	−8.52	4.14
1997	5,415,176	−1.11	227,447	0.28	4.20
1998	5,353,095	−1.15	209,789	−7.76	3.92
1999	5,374,751	0.40	210,113	0.15	3.91
2000	5,481,920	1.99	213,346	1.54	3.89
2001	5,632,936	2.75	218,695	2.51	3.88
2002	5,662,382	0.52	217,614	−0.49	3.84

Sources: http://www.bstubbs.co.uk/gcse.htm, http://www.qca.org.uk/, http://www.dfes.gov.uk/statistics/

in schools (NCC 1990; Speaker's Commission 1990; Fogelman 1991). At this stage, although national concerns about declining participation in the democratic process and in community life more generally were widespread, the impact of work on citizenship on practice in schools was limited. Following the 1997 election, the new Labour government established a more formal inquiry into citizenship education under the chairmanship of Bernard Crick; Crick had been a long-standing advocate of political education in schools (Crick and Porter 1978) and had also at one stage been David Blunkett's (the new Secretary of State) university politics tutor.

The Crick Report was clear, arguing that a fundamental responsibility of schools in a democratic society was to establish among learners the foundations for the practice of participatory citizenship (Crick 1998). While Crick argued that in

> History, there is much teaching and learning about the development of societies and of political and social and economic systems [while] the emphasis . . . on the use of evidence and processes of enquiry can help pupils to discuss and reach informed judgements about topical and contemporary issues.
>
> (Crick 1998: para. 73.7.4)

His committee proposed the establishment of citizenship with a 'distinct and separate articulation' in the secondary curriculum. Crick's rationale was that although citizenship education practice impinged on other subjects it also addressed specific issues in political education which might be diluted otherwise. Crick envisaged four interlocking components of citizenship education encompassing first, knowledge and understanding, second, key concepts and content, third, pedagogic practices and fourth, values and attitudinal development. For Crick, all four were essential; citizenship content depended on particular approaches to pedagogy and was designed to develop certain attitudes and values, including a disposition to active, participatory citizenship. Finally, Crick argued for a statutory entitlement to citizenship education, which would require schools to set aside time for the explicit teaching of citizenship: in effect a new statutory subject. The government largely adopted the Crick report and proposed the adoption of citizenship as an additional statutory national curriculum component from September 2002 at Key Stages 3 and 4. Crick's proposals, and the government's response to them, raised a series of challenges for history teachers, not least since the Advisory Group chaired by Crick had identified history in particular as the subject most suited to the delivery of elements of citizenship. Several commentators had argued that 'history education and education for citizenship . . . are . . . very similar in terms of meaning and purpose' (Davies 2001: 139; see also Slater and Hennessey 1978; Wrenn 2001). On the other hand, there have always been those who saw the 'use' of school history for citizenship education as a diversion from the central concern of history to develop understandings of the past (Bousted and Davies 1996). A second emerging issue for this study, then, is the impact of the implementation of citizenship practice on history in schools.

At the time of writing, the final strands of the Key Stage 3 Strategy – foundation subjects and ICT – are being 'rolled out' in schools. They join three other strands, English, mathematics and science, and two other cross-curricular strands, literacy and numeracy. The early years of secondary schooling have become one of the government's main priorities in education, based on a concern that gains in attainment in Key Stage 2 are not being sustained in Key Stage 3 (Furlong *et al.* 2000). The Strategy has been lavishly funded, with a total expenditure of £500 million forecast by the end of 2004. Large quantities of training materials, guidance booklets and subject frameworks have been distributed and Key Stage 3 Strategy consultants have been appointed across the country to work with schools, LEAs and Initial Teacher Training providers. The Strategy is intended to build on the successful rise in standards at Key Stage 2, particularly in literacy and numeracy, and enable schools to meet ambitious targets at the end of Year 9. It is expected that as a result of the Strategy, by 2004 75 per cent of 14-years-olds will achieve level 5 in English, mathematics and ICT and 70 per cent in science. By 2007, these targets increase by 10 per cent. The Strategy's main emphasis is on remedying the well-documented 'attainment dip' which occurs during Key Stage 3 (Galton and

Rudduck 1999; Schagen and Kerr 1999). It emphasizes transition from Key Stage 2 to 3 and provides 'catch-up' for lower attainers and 'booster' materials to prepare pupils for their SATs in Year 9. Most significantly, however, it advances a pedagogical model purportedly designed to deliver the national curriculum more effectively. Practitioners at secondary level are familiar with government control of content; they are much less familiar with attempts to shape the way they teach.

For foundation subjects in particular, the pedagogical model outlined in the Strategy is essentially generic and as in all Strategy material, there are certain characteristic features such as recommended lesson structure, objectives-led planning and an emphasis on formative assessment. The extent to which this generic model sits easily alongside the specific demands of a subject such as history is open to debate. The Strategy as a whole is theoretically non-statutory but there is a clear expectation that schools will at least consider its potential use and application in raising standards. A third issue for this study is therefore related to the likely impact of the Key Stage 3 Strategy on schools and in departments.

A final issue shaping the professional landscape for history teachers relates to the challenges posed by underlying shifts in secondary education. The national curriculum ushered in an era of sharply increased accountability in British schools. The publication of examination and test results, the introduction of regular Ofsted inspections, increased competition between schools and the introduction of performance management progressively sharpened the significance of management at school level (Chitty 2002). The context for school and departmental management was shifted fundamentally in the 1990s (Harris 1999). Some of the influences appear to have been wholly instrumental: schools became increasingly concerned with examination outputs, and particularly with working with pupils at the margins of performance indicators. School-level curriculum and management information developed rapidly in scope, scale and sophistication (Busher and Harris 1999). Schools became increasingly concerned about the relationship between curriculum structure and measurable examination outputs, which frequently resulted in reductions in curriculum time for history, or about the performance of sub-populations of pupils, which had implications for the involvement of some groups in parts of the curriculum and the culture of schooling (McMahon 2001). The preoccupation with outcome-led management posed a series of challenges for history teachers and perhaps particularly for heads of department. Just as the 11–14 curriculum was being reshaped around the priorities of the Key Stage 3 Strategy so, in some schools, 14–19 curriculum structures were being modified to enhance vocational components. As a result, history was under threat as an entitlement for all learners. This threat to history in the secondary curriculum appeared to be exacerbated by the introduction, following the 2001 White Paper on secondary education, of increasing numbers of specialist school categories, including technology, languages, business, mathematics, sports and performing arts, but not of humanities or history. Anecdotal evidence suggested the marginalization of history in schools which had developed specialisms in other areas. These large-scale shifts in the structure and assumptions of secondary education as a result of policy development nationally prompted a final research question: How were history teachers responding to the changed expectations and demands? The extent to which the curriculum and managerial challenges of the 1990s presented challenges to professional values and assumptions has been a theme of recent research (see, for example, Woods *et al.* 1997; Earley *et al.* 1998; Helsby 1999). This study examines the issues through the lens of history teaching.

History teaching has been repeatedly transformed over the last three decades by curriculum change – sometimes emerging from curriculum development work, sometimes from changed national expectations, sometimes from shifts in perception outside the subject about the focus of the curriculum and the nature of schooling. So much is clear. What is less clear is the ways in which these changes impact on teachers' own practice and their perceptions of their practice. For all the rhetorical bluster of the last three decades, we know precious little about the ways teachers have responded and adapted their classroom practice and their curriculum thinking. It is teachers' current practice which forms the central concern of this book.

2 Why research history teaching?

One way of ensuring that reading difficulties do not always get in the way of historical thinking is for teachers to emphasise the visual dimension. 'The visual image', wrote Unwin (1981) 'has largely replaced the written word as our principal means of communication'. Research by Rogers (1984) indicated that pupils of all abilities preferred working with visual material, which also helped their understanding.

(Farmer and Knight 1995: 41)

If children are to be encouraged to develop the ability to communicate in writing then they need to be helped: a blank piece of paper can be terribly daunting.

(Palmer, in Watts and Grosvenor 1995: 123)

Knowledge and understanding of historical interpretations are the weakest elements of learning in history. In some schools, work on interpretations takes place in a small number of focused units of work, such as interpretations of the origins of Rome, the kingship of John, or the religious beliefs of King Henry VIII. When this is successful, pupils understand that historical judgement is problematic, but many fail to transfer this principle to other units of work, or to learn different views of events, people and changes. Historical *interpretation* has a particular meaning in the National Curriculum, that is distinct from pupils' ability to *interpret* historical sources which, like other aspects of historical enquiry, is often good. At best, pupils apply learned skills to new situations, making good progress. In too many schools, however, opportunities for developing enquiry skills are limited, or not as good in one class as in another, and consequently there is little systematic development of such skills. Often these are schools where teaching is over-directive and insufficient attention is given to developing independent learning skills.

(Ofsted 2001)

Approaches to improving practice

We have seen, in the opening chapter, that the discipline of history teaching has undergone rapid and complex change over the past 30 years. The professional practices of history teachers have been transformed through a combination of extensive professional development, national policy intervention and curriculum development projects, aided by significant developments in both history as an academic subject and in education more generally. It is against this context that we want to understand history teaching in some detail, to consider the ways in which history teachers work and the implications of such work for understanding classrooms and teaching.

In dealing with the complexities of their professional duties, history teachers are not short of sources of advice and guidance. Staffroom library shelves fill with publications describing good or effective practices and offering instances of work undertaken by successful practitioners. Professional development programmes are replete with courses offered by successful practitioners, inspectors, advisers and academics. The examples quoted above are instances of such advice; at its best, it is rigorous and evidentially grounded, and at its very best it makes explicit its underlying assumptions about practice. However, such guidance frequently tends to beg a series of questions. The examples above – which are certainly good examples of their type – illustrate the difficulties. Guidance offered to practitioners is either overtly descriptive or overtly prescriptive.

The extract from the Ofsted report is an example of *descriptive* guidance, drawing as it does on the observations of history lessons carried out during inspection visits drawing on the *Ofsted Handbook for the Inspection of Schools*. Individual lessons are described on observation forms and are graded on the perceived effectiveness of the lesson within the guidance of the framework. Subject overview reports are based on a rigorous analysis of this descriptive data by Her Majesty's Inspectors, and seek to tease out classroom examples of effective practice which provide portmanteau guides for classroom teachers, as well as drawing attention to areas of general concern which emerge from an annual cycle of reports (see the example above). These summary accounts serve a valuable purpose in drawing together a wide range of inspection findings and alerting professionals and those who work with them to underlying issues of professional practice. But the accounts are limited by their reliance on disconnected descriptions of lessons which collect examples of 'outstanding', 'satisfactory' or 'poor' practice for the purposes of inspection.

They do not help to understand the ways in which the ingredients of professional practice are combined, nor the circumstances in which good and effective practice is likely to develop. Perhaps more important, there is an element of circularity in the description: the inspection framework outlines criteria for judgement, which form a sort of template for the accumulation of evidence against which practice is judged and from which the template is verified. The framework describes effective practice and inspectors and teachers set out to achieve this pattern of effective practice. As the government has become more concerned with strategies and interventions which recommend particular pedagogic practices, the range and quantity of such descriptive guidance on how history and other subjects should be taught has markedly increased.

The other type of guidance is overtly *prescriptive*. The examples quoted from Palmer and from Farmer and Knight at the beginning of this chapter are characteristic of the type: a model of good and effective practice is either implicitly or explicitly developed and classroom strategies which will overcome perceived difficulties in the implementation of this model are recommended, often with the aid of examples of lesson plans, teaching resources or pupils' work. In most cases, advice is legitimated both against examples of classroom practice and, as in the first instance we quote above, against a tradition of other propositional or research literature. There is a good deal of anecdotal evidence that teachers, both novice and experienced, find such prescriptive advice useful at a number of different stages in their development. Beginner teachers find the guidance a useful source of classroom strategies and 'tips' (Husbands and Pendry 2000). More experienced teachers frequently customize ideas and suggestions from these guides, and they are perhaps especially useful in mediating the implementation of particular externally imposed innovations (see, for example, Watts and Grosvenor, 1995) or in providing routes to addressing systemic issues in professional practice, such as teaching history to pupils with special educational needs (Wilson 1985; Clarke and Wrigley 1991), literacy (Counsell 1997) or multicultural dimensions of history teaching (Pankhania 1994). Again, then, prescriptive guidance – manuals for teaching – has an important role in the busy teacher's professional armoury and should not be decried. However, such prescriptive guidance seems to us to suffer from a number of underlying difficulties. The first of these is a tendency to *simplify* the complexities of professional practice and to regard the presenting difficulties of history teaching as separate rather than interlinked, for example, seeing literacy as separate from special needs. In this sense, the prescriptions do resemble medical prescriptions: focused interventions to address specific symptoms rather than more holistic attempts to describe difficulties and strategies in the context of professional complexity. The second difficulty relates to the underlying ideas about 'good practice' which frequently underpin such advice, whether good practice is associated with the use of evidence (Andreetti 1993), 'active' learning (Farmer and Knight 1995) or teacher reflection (Phillips 2002). In few cases are these conceptual-izations of good or effective practices rigorously grounded in *evidence-based* practice; the underlying ideas of good practice remain under-analysed and hence taken for granted (Alexander 1996) rather than being argued through in terms of a rigorously analysed evidence base.

Our approach in this book is different; we set out neither to be descriptive of effective practice nor prescriptive of good practice, but to explore a research agenda primarily concerned with understanding history teaching. We want to locate our understandings of history teaching and the ideas and practices of history teachers against a series of research contexts. Several points need to be made. The first is that we do not offer our research perspective as inherently superior to, or to supplant, either the descriptive work of policy-led and inspection-led work nor the prescriptive manuals focused on usable classroom strategies; instead we want to use research resources and a research perspective to illuminate the classroom practices which inevitably underpin descriptive and prescriptive approaches. Second, as will become apparent, we will argue that history teaching – and indeed subject teaching more generally – is a considerably under-researched phenomenon; our work does little more than establish some initial pointers which need further refinement. With this in mind, we turn to a consideration of the sorts of research which have already been deployed in the area, and the extent to which they are helpful in under-standing history teaching.

Researching children's understanding of history

Perhaps the largest body of research in the area of history education is that which relates to children's understanding in history. While this work has focused on children's and adolescent's thinking, some elements of the work have had powerful impacts on teaching strategies and curriculum con-struction. Early work in the field, carried out by Peel (1960, 1966), Coltham and Fines (1970) and Hallam (1975) was heavily influenced by the Swiss psychologist Jean Piaget. Piaget had outlined a stage theory of children's cognitive development, moving from 'concrete' to 'formal operational' and 'abstract' conceptualizations (Inhelder and Piaget 1958), and much early history education research was concerned with identifying patterns of development in children's thinking which allowed them to deploy forms of abstract and logical reasoning on which an understanding of the past developed (Peel 1966; Coltham and Fines 1970). Peter Lee and Ros Ashby have pointed out that while such early work was carried out within a largely Piagetian framework, in practice the outcomes of such work involved a recognition that Piaget's views on children's inability to understand the past were unduly pessimistic and that his theories were in need of considerable modification (Lee and Ashby 2001).

Two major research contributions broke the grip of Piagetian influence on children's understanding of the past. The first was that of Martin Booth (1979, 1987), who argued in a series of trenchant studies that Piagetian work had had a 'restricting effect on the history curriculum and our ideas about the development of children's historical understanding' (Booth 1987: 26). Booth was explicitly concerned with exploring the relationship between children's thinking and the development of 'teaching strategies which can help to raise our expectations of children's potential' (1987: 28). Booth explored the ways in which adolescent pupils used evidential materials to engage in what he called 'genuine historical thinking', and he coined a useful neologism to describe the cognitive processes he observed in the way his study pupils grouped and analysed historical material – he called it 'adductive' historical reasoning, and concluded that 'pupils of a wide range of abilities and ages can engage in proper history; teaching for particular skills and understandings can and does make a difference' (1987: 31). But, warned Booth, it was necessary for teaching to 'consciously determine . . . objectives and teaching methods in the light of our understanding of what history is' (1987: 32). Booth extrapolated from his work with students to the explicit recommendation of the capacity of 'exploratory, open-ended exercises . . . to [support pupils'] ability to get to grips with complex abstract ideas' (Booth 1987: 33, 38). In the late 1970s and early 1980s, Booth's work had a powerful impact on teacher thinking and on syllabus construction at a time of rapid curriculum development.

The second major contribution which transcended Piagetian constraints on thinking about children's understanding grew out of Denis Shemilt's evaluation of the Schools' Council History Project (SHP) (Shemilt 1980). In a series of papers Shemilt drew on the extensive interview data collected for the SHP study to outline robust models for progression in adolescents' ideas about causation (Shemilt 1987), empathy (Shemilt 1984; Lee and Ashby 1987) and evidence and methodology (Shemilt 1987). Where Booth's work supported a focus on the construction of classroom tasks, there is strong evidence from the impact on assessment practice at examination boards (SREB 1986) of the direct influence of Shemilt's (1987) work on thinking about progression in the understanding of procedural historical concepts. Taking Shemilt's (1987) paper on evidence and methodology as an example, he showed how adolescents conceptually displayed progressively more sophisticated ideas about historical method. At what he called Stage 1, knowledge of the past is taken for granted. At this stage pupils are unable to offer more than 'bizarre and inappropriate answer to the question "How do we know?" ' (Shemilt 1987: 44); at Stage 2, pupil thinking is characterized by the realization 'that historical truth is negotiable' (1987: 50), and that historians need to make some use of evidence to construct what are regarded as 'true and accurate' pictures of the past. At Stage 3, evidence is seen as a basis for inference about the past, evidence and information are differentiated and learners realize that the historian uses evidence to draw inferences about the past which may be more or less reliable: 'conclusions are . . . inferred rather than read off from sources' (1987: 52). Finally, at Stage 4 – the most sophisticated thinking Shemilt found among SHP pupils, pupils are 'aware of the historicity of evidence' (1987: 56): written history is recognized as a reconstruction of past events which involves profound methodological difficulties and the possibility of multiple interpretations. Shemilt's work, like Booth's, was linked to powerful implications for the thinking and practice of history teachers, in particular here, on the presentation of 'background information', which, argued Shemilt, 'should always be presented as secondary source material and never as extra-evidential data' (1987: 60). Equally important, the articulation of a history-specific model of progression in terms of elements of historical understanding focused the attention of practitioners on both ideas of progression generally, but more specifically on the issues involved in enhancing the progression of students from one stage to the next and, crucially, on the relationship between written classroom activities and assessment practice. Shemilt's work provided the first real basis for developing conceptions of interpretations of history as an integral component of thinking about children's progression in the subject. 'Perhaps', comments Lee, 'the greatest importance of the work has been as a means of helping raise the level of teachers' own ideas' (Lee 1998: 3).

Since the work of Booth and Shemilt, work on children's understanding of history has been developed by Peter Lee, Alaric Dickinson and Rosalyn Ashby, all associated with the London Institute of Education, both through the Economic and Social Research Council (ESRC) funded CHATA (Concepts of History and Teaching Approaches) project and through a series of studies undertaken by research students under their supervision (Dickinson and Lee 1994). Ashby and Lee (1987) initially developed a systematic model for mapping progression in children's ideas about empathy, logging a progression from what they called conceptions of the 'divi' past in which people in the past were held to be generally ill-informed and ignorant, to a subtle 'differentiated empathy' where children were able to understand the differences and similarities within and between people in the past (Ashby and Lee 1987).

In other respects, the London work has moved away from the critical connections made by Booth and Shemilt between adolescents' ideas and teaching approaches to map in greater detail elements of children's tacit understandings of historical accounts between the ages of 7 and 14. Project CHATA concluded that learners can acquire important and significant ideas about historical accounts from the age of 7, and generally linked patterns of progression in these understandings to age-related progression. However, while firming up models of progression, Ashby, Lee and Dickinson (1996) concluded that general patterns of progression do not describe individual learning paths: they are not ladder-like, with students moving from one step to the next. Students may jump steps and behave differently with different questions as well as with different content. Increasingly, research students working within the CHATA tradition have explored the intriguing and complex questions of the cultural specificity of patterns of progression, with comparative studies of the development of conceptions of significance in English and Spanish pupils (Cercadillo 1998) and the ideas of Taiwanese students about the past (Hsaio 2002). Paradoxically therefore, in describing the complexities underlying the development of children's thinking, Ashby, Lee and Dickinson (1996) found it increasingly difficult to develop clear implications for teacher thinking and development from their research paradigm. Rich though CHATA has been, its largely experimental methodology has made it difficult to tease out professional applications of the work. Indeed, Lee has concluded that 'an essential focus for new work is teacher understandings and ideas' (Lee 1998: 5). In recent years, research in the United States has similarly focused on students' historical understanding. Two ideas have dominated much of this work: the nature of historical thinking engaged in by pupils, and the social and cultural contexts that may shape their thinking. Hence, for example, Barton (2001) has explored the ways in which children in Northern Ireland and the USA have very different conceptions of the purposes of learning in history, conceptions that are informed by the specific histories – and perceived needs – of those countries. Similarly Levstik (2000) has investigated adolescents' understandings of historical significance and demonstrates how their thinking is shaped by both the nature of the history of their country and by their desires for the future. Sam Wineburg (2001) has conducted a series of studies designed to discover both what is intrinsic to historical thinking and what it looks like in experts and novices and, most recently, to understand the ways in which this thinking is shaped by family, society and collective memory – so too has Peter Seixas (1996), in his exploration of what constitutes historical understanding and how it is shaped and developed.

What emerges then from work on children's understanding of history is a complex and rich understanding of the ways in which children develop progressively more complex understandings both of the procedural concepts of history (evidence, causation, significance, change, empathy) and of the interrelationship between these accounts and the construction of knowledge about the past. The research tradition, although increasingly concerned to unpack the complexity of children's thinking, has developed robust and powerful conceptualizations which inform professional practice. Booth's (1979) concept of 'adductive' historical thinking and its influence on the construction of open-ended classroom tasks, Lee and Ashby's (1987) work on patterns in the historical (as opposed to Rogerian) concept of empathy and its influence on teachers' conceptualizations of student's thinking, and

Shemilt's (1984, 1987) mapping of adolescents' understanding of methodology and evidence are all rich resources which might inform an exploration of the relationship between teacher thinking about history and teacher classroom practice. On its own, however, this research tradition leaves a great deal unexplored. There has been comparatively little interest in the relationships between the construction of classroom tasks and the construction of curricula, and relatively little interest in the ways in which teachers relate ideas about children's understandings to their own classroom practice.

Researching the purposes of history teaching

A second significant body of research is more philosophical in nature, relating to the purposes of history teaching in schools. The general aims of history teaching in schools have been sharply contested, both in the UK and internationally (for example, see Reeves 1980; Slater 1995; Dilek 1998; Phillips 1998; Bage 2001). At the root of these debates, there is a sense that history, of all school subjects, is the most controversial, encompassing as it does implied assumptions about values and principles and about national identity. In many countries there are explicit assumptions that the principal purpose of history in schools is to introduce children to, and by implication induct children into, particular views of the national culture (Ferro 1984). These debates reflect a number of different perspectives: the perspectives of government and politicians; the perspectives of administrators, inspectors and professionals; the perspectives of employers; the perspectives of parents; and the perspectives – though rarely explicitly elicited – of pupils.

In the United Kingdom, the introduction of a national curriculum and the establishment by the government of a government-picked working group to select the content for the national curriculum in history led to extensive national debate, pursued in conferences, think-tank pamphlets and in parliament; as Rob Phillips and others have shown such debates revealed starkly different assumptions about the nature and purposes of school history teaching (Phillips 1998). The Czech novelist Milan Kundera expressed some of the reasons for this debate sardonically:

> People are always shouting that they want to create a better future. It's not true. The future is an apathetic void of no interest to anyone. The past is full of eager life, there to irritate, provoke and insult us, tempt us to destroy it or repaint it. The only reason people want to be masters of the future is to change the past. They are fighting for access to the laboratories where photographs are retouched and biographies and history re-written.
>
> (Kundera 1982, quoted in Husbands, 1996: 135)

Looking back over the acres of press and professional reporting of dispute about the purposes of history in the national curriculum – debate to which two of the authors of this book contributed – one is struck by how ferocious some of the debate was and how little light it genuinely shed on the relationships between school history teaching and the wider purposes of teaching history in schools. In essence, the debate about the national curriculum was a political debate engendered by a political intervention, between, at the extremes, those who argued strenuously that the curriculum should be a vehicle for the transmission of a common cultural heritage, and, by implication, in an increasingly diverse society, for re-asserting that common cultural heritage (Tate 1995), and those at the other extreme who saw the core of school history as the development of 'historical thinking', which has a 'compensatory and oppositional function. It [may] compensate . . . and counter . . . the influence of the myth makers and inventors of tradition' (Slater 1995: 130).

More sophisticated discussions of the aims and purposes of school history can be found in the research literature where the issues of the purposes, aspirations and aims of history in schools have been more systematically explored. One of the most elegant and insightful discussions is offered by John Slater (1989), who draws an important distinction between what he calls the 'extrinsic' and 'intrinsic' purposes of school history. *Intrinsic* purposes are those sometimes represented as the learning of history 'for its own sake', though Slater questions the value of the term in defining what is at stake. Intrinsic aims chiefly emerge from concepts and assumptions within the discipline itself. Intrinsic objectives for school students might include the ability to distinguish between BC and AD, or to understand and to be able to give some account of the causes of the French Revolution. Such objectives derive from the view that the learning of history is itself intrinsically important, an element in what Richard Pring has elsewhere called 'the community of educated people' (Pring 1995). On the other hand, history may have *extrinsic* aims: 'to develop tolerance', 'to develop an understanding of a shared culture', 'to develop the abilities to participate in a participatory democracy' and so on. These aims, notes Slater (1995: 126) 'are concerned with changing society', and they are 'broader *educational* aims', and, however significant, they are 'not historical', even though 'broader extrinsic educational aims may well help us select issues which will then be studied with intrinsic historical procedures'. This lucid distinction casts considerable light on the dispute about school history teaching which underpinned the introduction of the national curriculum but remained unresolved – and could not have been resolved given its political nature – after it. Slater (1995) goes on to argue that it might be possible to make further distinctions between intrinsic aims which the teaching of history might seek to guarantee – we might aspire to *guarantee* that all students learn to use dating corrections correctly, but can only *enable* students to become more tolerant, more civic-minded and so on.

From these distinctions Slater proceeds to distinguish seven different functions of history in school of which the first three and the last derive predominantly from the intrinsic purposes of history, the fifth and sixth from the extrinsic purposes of history and the fourth has, in different ways, relationships to both intrinsic and extrinsic purposes of history (Slater 1995). We use these functions to explore the philosophical debates around school history. *First*, he argued, drawing on Collingwood, 'history is "for" human self-knowledge . . . Knowing yourself means knowing first what it means to be a man' (*sic*, p. 129). For Collingwood, history's function lay precisely in the understandings of different ways of thinking – all history, he famously observed, is the history of thought (Pring 1995). Slater developed this aspect of the function of history by arguing that 'history gives us our individual, cultural and national identities' (1995: 127). More recently, discussions of school history have explored the complexities of developing this function of history education in a rapidly changing, culturally diverse society where cultural inheritances are themselves contested subjects and where the extent to which an inclusive history of a diverse nation can be explored within a common national curriculum have been debated (Pankhania 1994; Grosvenor 2000). Grant Bage, in a deeply-felt and argued piece identifies the complexities of this 'self-knowledge' in shifting community *locales*, beginning by exploring a case study of bilingual learners in an East London school where the cultural inheritances draw on African, Caribbean, Jewish, Irish and French migration and where local, national and international identities are themselves forged through the richness of cultural diversity: 'perhaps the cleverest educational response to cultural diversity and systemic globalisation is to build from the local outwards, to offer communities access to the best and most diverse of the national' (Bage 2001: 148).

Second, Slater (1995) characterizes 'history . . . [a]s the never ending pursuit of cause and explanation . . . facts alone never explain or justify' (p. 127). *Third*, history is for reducing 'our misunderstanding and ignorance of the world by placing it into contexts of change' (p. 128). These two functions derive particularly from the intrinsic purposes of history; both are propositions about the outcomes of particular engagements with historical contexts, but, equally, provide a values framework for addressing these contexts. Most recently the power of such models to stimulate teacher thinking have been explicitly demonstrated through professionally focused publications which demonstrate that conceptualizations of content can support powerful outcomes in terms of pupils' historical and wider understanding. Dale Banham's (1998) study of an engagement with material around King John, and Michael Riley's (1997) work on the relationship between 'overview' and 'depth' studies both demonstrate the significance of relating historical content to a clearly articulated sense of the relationships between knowledge, causation and explanation.

Fourth, argues Slater, 'history supplies us with procedures for authenticating statements made about other human beings' (1995: 128). There is a significant linkage here in Slater's argument, connecting concerns which in much discourse about the subject in schools are treated separately, namely 'evidential understanding' and 'historical empathy'. Conservative philosophers of history since Elton (1969) had been suspicious of both, since they appeared to place a premium on provisional and individual responses to historical material rather than on the acquisition of canonical knowledge about them. Nonetheless, the evidential basis of school history and the recourse to evidence to justify and authenticate statements of opinion and interpretation remains one of the aspects which connects intrinsic to extrinsic models of the discipline: for Beverley Labbett (1979) it was this evidential aspect almost alone which provided the basis for a curriculum specification for history. The dangers in this approach – the need to supplement evidence with 'imagination, explanation and understanding' (Dickinson, Gard and Lee, 1978: 17) – provide the linkage to the focus of historical statements on 'other human beings' and the linkage to empathetic approaches to the past. These are complex territories, where mis-specifications at the level of aims produce sharply problematic practices in classrooms, but equally where the clarity of conceptualization of the difficulties is essential if conditions are to be established for effective professional practice (for example, see SREB 1986).

Fifth, argues Slater, history has 'a compensatory oppositional function' (1995: 130), a view of history which reaches back to E.P. Thompson's powerful aspiration to 'give a voice to the voiceless' (Thompson 1965). We have already seen that this oppositional function was prominent in debates over the introduction of the national curriculum. For the socialist historian, Raphael Samuel (1994), writing at the time of the debates over the content of the national curriculum and afterwards, this 'oppositional function' was to be discharged by engaging with a popular memory tradition of radical popular patriotism, which needed to be articulated through an engagement with the myth-making that invariably underlay high culture versions of national history. Such claims were particularly pointed in the United Kingdom in the late 1980s. At that time, a Conservative government was under sustained pressure from right-wing pressure groups and Conservative MPs to ensure that British history, and in particular Britain's political, constitutional and cultural heritage was at the core of the history national curriculum (Phillips 2000). Slater himself was highly critical of what he saw as inevitable attempts by the government to exclude this compensatory purpose of history. In his special professorial lecture at London Institute in 1988, delivered at the inception of the national curriculum, he argued that

> if history does not guarantee attitudes and aspirations it is a necessary
> if not a sufficient condition which might enable the making of

informed choices. It cannot guarantee tolerance though it may give it some intellectual weapons. It cannot keep open closed minds though it may, sometimes leave a nagging grain of doubt in them. Historical thinking is primarily mind-opening, not socialising.

(Slater 1988: 16)

Sixth, Slater describes history's part in laying the foundations for non-vocational lifelong learning, 'for satisfying curiosity, developing leisure interests and for offering pure enjoyment' (1995: 132). This aspiration of school history receives little emphasis in disputes about the purposes of school history. One of us has noted elsewhere (Husbands 1996) the extent to which the mass media has become increasingly preoccupied with the historical past and the enormous popularity of representations of the past. The SHP's prospectus document, *A New Look at History* (Schools' Council 1976) placed what was then seen as a central preoccupation – the need to prepare young people for the expected growth in leisure time – at the centre of its aspirations for history in school. In practice, however, more recent discussions of the relationship between history and lifeskills have developed differently and have tended to examine ways in which history might thrive in an increasingly vocationally focused curriculum. Indeed, one interpretation of the obsession with the underpinning skills of history teaching which dominate discourse in the two decades after the publication of the SHP prospectus was that it connected precisely to the need for history to demonstrate its contributions to a work-related curriculum; Christine Counsell (2000b) has lucidly explored the difficulties which arise from a focus which defines the subject solely in terms of the generic and specific skills it develops.

Finally, *seventh*, suggests Slater, history is for 'recording the diversity and complexity of human achievement . . . "the peaks, the depths, the banality and the contradictions" of human behaviour' (1995: 132). Wineburg discusses the ways in which 'mature historical knowing teaches us to . . . go beyond our brief life and the brief moment in human history into which we've been born. History educates ("leads outward" in Latin)' (Wineburg 2001: 14). More recent philosophers of history have encountered considerable difficulties with this openly humanistic statement of the purpose of studying the past. Notably, Keith Jenkins (1991), drawing on post-modern perspectives, has posed questions about historical discourse as a mode of reasoning. Jenkins wants to place much greater emphasis on the ways in which history as an account of the past is constructed and is therefore different from the past. He questions the extent to which it is possible for history to educate about human behaviour in the past rather than about the historians who have constructed accounts of the past.

We have used Slater's analysis as the basis for a review of work on the aims and purposes of school history. In doing so, we have explored rich distinctions between underlying philosophical observations. Several issues of relevance to the study of the practice of history teachers emerge. The first is almost truistic: the aims of history teaching are contested not simply in political terms (where questions about the political control of the curriculum and its relationship to an over-arching hegemonic culture remain contested) but also in more strictly educational terms. Second, we have observed that there are legitimate tensions between general educational aims and specifically historical aims of school history; we have learnt that the aims of teaching history rest within and are contingent upon wider educational aims and aspirations. Third, we have explored a variety of expressed functions for the school history curriculum and observed the richness and complexity of underlying assumptions about the discipline in school. Fourth, we have raised post-modern questions about whether history as a mode of discourse can sustain the demands placed upon it. All this advances our understanding of the intellectual and philosophical discourse within which school history teachers are located, and casts light on the purposes of the discipline. We should expect that different teachers in different contexts will reflect to differing degrees elements of debate around Slater's seven functions of school history. But one interesting element of the discussion has been the absence from the debate of the voices of history teachers themselves. Illuminating and useful though the debates are in the extent to which they point up areas of debate, tension and disagreement, they do not, in general, engage with the lived professional practice of teachers, although Phillips (2002) has recently argued powerfully for the centrality of history teachers' reflection on history teaching as a key element in driving forward the practice of the discipline.

Researching teaching

A third significant research tradition focuses on teachers and classroom teaching. In the late 1960s, when Martin Booth conducted fieldwork for his ground-breaking study, *History Betrayed?*, the practice of classroom teachers was relatively under-researched. Over the three decades since, of course, increasing amounts of research effort has been devoted to understanding classroom teaching and, perhaps increasingly, to prescribing changes in classroom practice. However, relatively little of this research has attempted to explore issues of classroom teaching in relation to history. We have already noted a significant strain of such research-derived professional writing which sets out to tell teachers how to teach, but we have noted the extent to which its commitment to prescribe particular approaches, in frequently decontextualized and over-simplified ways makes it a poor tool for normative directions to analytical understandings. What remains unclear from the prescriptive literature is the extent to which it relates to lived classroom practice.

For this reason, we need to look elsewhere for evidence of usable research on history teaching.

Researchers in the United States initially led the field in researching history teaching. In the 1980s the focus was on what was termed pedagogical content knowledge. Shulman (1986), who coined the term, described this as:

> For the most regularly taught topics in one's subject area, the most useful forms of representation of those ideas, the most powerful analogies, illustrations, examples, explanations and demonstration – in a word, ways of representing and formulating the subject that makes it comprehensible to others. Pedagogical content knowledge also includes an understanding of what makes the learning of specific topics easy or difficult; the conceptions and preconceptions that students of different ages and backgrounds bring with them to the learning of those most frequently taught topics and lessons.
>
> (pp. 9–10)

Case studies of individual teachers (see, for example, Gudmundsdottir and Shulman 1989; Wilson 1990; Wilson and Wineburg, 1991) looked at the ways in which both beginning and expert teachers transformed their own knowledge of history into a form accessible to their learners. They looked at the ways in which, for example, teachers' different conceptions of the discipline of history impacted on their teaching of the subject (Wilson and Wineburg 1988) and the ways in which history teachers' beliefs and values influenced the ways in which they taught the subject (Gudmundsdottir 1991). This work has helped us to recognize the significance of subject matter in teacher expertise and more recently Brophy and Van Sledright (1997) conducted case studies of three American high school teachers and their fifth grade students to explore the relationships between teacher ideas and practices and the students' learning of history. The utility and relevance of this work to understanding history teachers in the UK context may, however, be limited: much of the work has been based on American social studies teaching, where subject knowledge issues present themselves differently and where there is a less well developed context for professional discourse around the development of the subject. Additionally, the American research has been strongly influenced by two linked imperatives: that the starting point in making sense of history teaching must be an account of the discipline provided by philosophers of history and, second, that what teachers in the US *should* do is attend more to the nature of their subject. Hence, this research strays into the territory of the prescriptive guidance discussed earlier. Nonetheless, it does alert us to some potentially important dimensions of history teachers' expertise and especially the value of their own understandings of history.

There are two more developed bodies of work on teaching which may be useful. 'It can sometimes seem', observe Brown and McIntyre (1993: 2), 'that the history of research on teaching is simply one of changing fashions, with each new generation of researchers neglecting the work of their predecessors and concentrating their attention on new questions'. Two recent studies are of particular importance, although they develop from contrasting perspectives. Cooper and McIntyre (1996) explored the interactions of secondary school teachers with their classes to unpack the perceived components of effective teaching in relation to learning, drawing on teacher accounts and, to a lesser extent, pupil perspectives. Their work offered a rich analysis of the lesson 'grammars' which teachers associated with 'preferred working states' and directed attention to the sophistication of teacher actions in bringing about learning in classrooms. Increasingly, research has been concerned to identify the components of effective teaching which can be translated into policy interventions and improvement programmes (for example, Hay McBer 2000). Among the most influential of recent studies is that by Muijs and Reynolds. Muijs and Reynolds (2001) focus on the observed behaviours of teachers which can be associated with effective learning in a range of contexts – particularly, but not exclusively, in the acquisition of key basic skills such as literacy and numeracy. For Muijs and Reynolds, the deployment of effective behaviours is a highly skilled technical accomplishment encompassing planning, management and assessment skills, and they lay enormous stress on teacher skill in decision making under pressure in choosing the patterns of interventions which will impact on learner effectiveness. Unlike some theorists of teacher effectiveness, Muijs and Reynolds (2001) see effective teaching as a product of high, rather than routinized, technical skills, and their work is useful in alerting us to the complexity of the classroom skills with which we are dealing. In two crucial areas, however, they leave elements of our concerns unexamined. In the first place, they are relatively uninterested in the knowledge which underpins the way teachers behave: beyond their work on literacy and numeracy, they make relatively little of curriculum content. This reflects a wider tendency in teacher effectiveness studies to concentrate on the acquisition of basic, rather than complex, skills and may raise more fundamental doubts about the model. In the second place, they appear to be comparatively uninterested in the values framework of teachers; again, in the context of their study this makes sense, but, in the context of the sophisticated functions which Slater (1995) explores for history, it raises questions about the interplay between technical skills, subject knowledge and value systems.

Some of this interplay has been explored in work on other subject areas, and particularly in work on the teaching of science and mathematics. We want to explore two pieces of work. In an insightful study of the ways in which science teachers explain science in the classroom, Jon Ogborn and his colleagues (1996) explored four main tasks undertaken by science teachers:

opening up difference, constructing entities, transforming knowledge and making matter meaningful, which in the hands of skilful teachers 'all happen together at the same time'. They claim that describing the structure of explanations in this way, and illustrating the complexities of explanation, provides a basis for understanding teaching: in their words 'naming is half-way to recognising and recognising is half way to thinking again' (Ogborn *et al.* 1996: 83). In some respects, Ogborn and his colleagues have a similar concern to ours here: to unpack the ways in which teachers work and to do so by examining their practice in depth by focusing on a relatively small number of instances. Their work is useful in both highlighting the importance of the strategies deployed to build explanations, and in demonstrating the ways in which experienced teachers use multiple communication structures simultaneously. Concern with understanding the basis of teaching practices has been explored in the context of mathematics education by Kenneth Ruthven (1999). Just as ideas about history education practice were transformed by the Schools' History Project, so ideas about mathematics education practice were transformed in the early 1980s by the Cockcroft Report, which articulated a strongly normative model of 'good practice' (Cockcroft 1982). This 'good practice' received strong official endorsement from HMI and from the early mathematics national curriculum, but, argues Ruthven, it had only limited impact on classroom practice: 'it is this predominance of advocacy and authority over argument which is the central problem of any idea of "good practice" ' (Ruthven 1999: 204). Ruthven traces two other strongly influential trends in recent discourse on mathematics education, what he calls the 'subjectivism of "reflective practice" and the . . . empiricism of "effective practice" ' (Ruthven 1999: 207). The former places a high premium on teacher personal experience and reflection, while the latter places a premium on the identification of efficient and effective strategies for achieving particular measurable outcomes. Ruthven, while acknowledging the strengths of each of these conceptions – 'good', 'reflective' and 'effective' practice – argues that 'sustained improvement and professional accountability in school mathematics call for a reconstruction of professional judgement on a more adequate – and more explicit epistemological base: to create . . . warranted practice' (Ruthven 1999: 209). Askew and Wiliam have reported elsewhere 'how little British research there is on important issues in teaching and learning [in mathematics]' (Askew and Wiliam 1995: 7), and Ruthven sketches out a set of procedural principles for the 'warranting of practice', based around clear operational models for practice grounded on 'continuing analysis and revaluation of the operational model in the light of evidence from . . . practice . . . and professional knowledge' (Ruthven 1999: 210).

Conclusion

In this chapter we have explored three research traditions and their relevance to understanding the professional practice of history teachers. We have argued that much of the current literature in the United Kingdom is either prescriptive or descriptive, and offered a critique of both tendencies. We have found three research traditions partially helpful: we have identified ways in which research on children's understanding of history can shape teacher sensitivities to the organization and selection of content and learning strategies, but too often found that the experimental method of research into children's understanding of history limited its utility as a tool for analysing teaching – a limitation its proponents readily accept. We have examined the ways in which a rich vein of discourse about the purposes of history teaching sensitizes us to the potential richness of classroom and professional practice, and how far removed this has been from the crudities of political and popular debate on the aims of history teaching. Finally, we have explored research into teaching, noting that useful insights developed by American researchers rest too much on the particular curricular and professional traditions of America to be readily transportable, before finding useful conceptual tools in two UK research traditions beyond history teaching. From contrasting work on teacher practice, we identify the sophistication of teachers' classroom skills as a fruitful area for exploration, but wish to underpin it with what was strongest in the American research tradition: a focus on knowledge and its relation to pedagogy.

3   How was this book researched?

Windows on practice

We move from the professional and research contexts in which history teaching is conventionally practised to a study of the practice itself. We begin with three brief visits to classrooms across England.

It's Monday morning. In a comprehensive school in England, lessons begin. Pupils have already spent about 15 minutes in pastoral form groups where they are logged into the electronic register and swap their weekend news, and they now move about the school to the first formal academic lesson of the day. A mixed ability form group of 12-year-olds assemble to begin their week's work with a history lesson. They enter the room, find their seats and, for the most part, though not all expeditiously, take out the equipment they will need for the 50-minute lesson: pens, pencils and exercise books. Their history teacher calls them to order and begins by taking the register. The lesson begins. It opens with a question and answer session about Thomas à Becket. Pupils are asked some questions about the previous lesson, about its content and their own awareness of the learning outcomes. The teacher, with the practised professional skill of someone who has done this for a long time, steers the questioning about church and state in the Middle Ages towards a discussion of state, government and kingship, until he can draw the class together and identify both the topic for today's lesson and the learning outcomes he expects: by the end of the lesson, pupils will have found out what Magna Carta was and identified its significance for the role of government in the Middle Ages. These overall aims for today's lesson are logged on the whiteboard, and pupils enter into their exercise books the date, the title for today's work ('Magna Carta') and a note of the objectives of the lesson ('1 To find out what Magna Carta was. 2 To understand the significance of Magna Carta in the Middle Ages'). The teacher asks the pupils to open their textbooks, and reads a translation of Clause 39 of Magna Carta. 'This is important', he says, 'listen carefully'.

By this time on the same Monday morning, 200 miles away, another history lesson, this time with a mixed ability group of 15-year-olds and a different history teacher, has also got a lesson under way. The topic is different: the class are examining the way in which Mao Zhe Dong regrouped the Chinese communist party on the Long March. The focus is on the tensions between how Lenin's assumptions about the urban basis of Marxism were challenged in the Chinese countryside. A week ago, the teacher had explained to the group that they would be completing a piece of coursework for their GCSE examinations explaining the reasons for the Chinese communist party's triumph in 1949. Over the succeeding lessons, the class will explore different explanatory factors. On file paper, they have a chart which they are completing over these lessons: one box looking at the failings of the KMD and Chiang Kai Shek has already been completed, and this lesson examines the second box on the chart – the role of ideology in the rise of the communist party. The class work from a school produced worksheet, which presents a series of short extracts, between 30 and 80 words long, from Leninist and Maoist tracts. A textbook, showing a map of the Long March is open on each desk. The teacher, like his counterpart in the Year 8 lesson, works through skilled question and answer. He directs pupils to passages on the worksheet, asks questions to establish understandings of meaning and reminds pupils of the historical context. There is an insistent line in his questioning: repeatedly, like a mantra he asks them: 'How does this help us to explain why the communist party won support?' Another text. Then the same question, 'How does this help us to explain why the communist party won support?' And so on, focusing always on this underlying question of causation which feeds into the question underlying the coursework assignment, and also feeding in his own interpretations: 'For my money, Mao was quite right to do this, very skilful, but it isn't clear whether he was simply using the ideas of Lenin or whether he did believe them. What do you think, Laura? Now, how does that help us to explain why the communist party won support?'

It's almost 10 o'clock now; in the first school, the bell marking the end of the first lesson is about to go, but in a third school, a third history teacher is halfway through a double lesson with a group of eight 17-year-olds. They sit around a small square of tables. To the left of the teacher is a video player and a large television set. She has just turned off the television set having shown the class very brief extracts from two television documentaries about the Italian Renaissance.

> I want to give you a couple of minutes alone to jot down differences between the interpretations of the role of Florence in the Renaissance which you took from those two extracts; then compare your notes in two ways – first, compare your list with your neighbour, and then look at the extract you have from Burkhardt. It's a classic of historical

interpretation, but it's now very dated. I want you to see whether either of the programmes still draws on Burkhardt. Two minutes alone, then five minutes in pairs.

The students jot down ideas. One asks for clarification, 'The first programme wasn't just about Florence, was it? How important is that?, and is deflected, 'Well, think about the claims which all three, Burkhardt, the first programme and the second programme appear to be making.' After 7 minutes, the teacher draws the class together and asks them to identify the similarities and differences in interpretations before moving on to consider the influence of Burkhardt's classic nineteenth-century work on popular representations of the Renaissance. With 10 minutes to go, she passes out a copy of a more recent interpretation, this time by Peter Burke. 'This is a view which is radically different from that of Burkhardt, and I remember coming across this when I was a student – it is very much a sociological interpretation. Read it through now and ask me for any clarifications you need, then I am going to want you to write about 500 words comparing the interpretations of the role of Florence in the Renaissance. You'll need to be able to develop your abilities to analyse historical interpretations as we move through the AS syllabus.'

Three lessons. One way of looking at these lessons is to see them, as it were, as the peak of an iceberg, sitting on the insights we have so far culled from the professional and research contexts against which classroom practice is enacted. Thus, in all three lessons, pupils are presented with artefacts – a text book, extracts from primary historical sources, videos, historical writing. The ways in which they make sense of these documents draws on the work of researchers on pupils' understanding of historical evidence, on the curriculum specifications set out in the national curriculum or examination requirements, and so on. The practice in this way is understood in the light of the wider context on which it rests. However, in each case, the lesson was the result of a further refracting lens – the lens of the history teacher and his or her views about the discipline of history and the contexts which we have already described. It is this lens which we want to understand, to examine the ways in which lessons, and these learners' experiences, are shaped by the teachers' understanding of the task they face. On the evidence presented above, it is difficult to advance arguments about this. In each lesson there are active engagements on the part of the teacher with historical interpretation – the importance of Clause 39 of Magna Carta, the views of Mao and Maoism, the views on Burke's interpretations of the Renaissance. But if we want to understand the interplay between the curriculum, the classroom and the history teacher, we need to dig deeper. In particular, we need to explore teacher perceptions and teacher practice, and above all, the ways in which teachers describe their professional practices in the light of the pressures they perceive.

Exploring professional practice

Our concern then is to explore the rationales for, and practices of, school history teaching in different settings. Our principal focus is on the ways in which history teachers make connections and forge relationships between their understandings of the discipline and its intellectual traditions, expectations set out in curriculum specifications, their perceptions of pupil needs and the school context. These considerations can be seen as both resources and constraints for the construction of effective learning in classrooms, and if we want to understand the way in which that learning is effected then we need to establish patterns of relationship between them.

The data which underlies this book are derived from an empirical study of history teaching in English comprehensive schools originally funded by the Nuffield Foundation. The Nuffield study explored the teaching of history in eight English comprehensive schools and a detailed account of the methodology is set out in the Appendix. In each school we set out to explore the relationship between the aims and objectives of the history curriculum and the day-to-day practice and articulation of that practice by history teachers. In order to explore practice, we collected data in each school in three ways. First of all, we observed one member of the history department at work over a full day's lessons. The decision to observe over a full day was deliberate. There is an extensive and legitimate debate in qualitative research about the extent to which it is possible to capture the typical and the everyday. By observing over a full day, normally involving between four and seven lessons, we were able to capture two things. The first was a range of teaching contexts across the full range of the English secondary school, from work with 11-year-olds through to work with 18-year-olds. The second was a sense of the daily rhythm of teaching: by the end of the day, each of our teachers was tired. Had we observed our study teachers with a single class over a series of weeks, we might have built up more evidence about pupil progression and the ways teachers planned for it, but our presence would have been more of an event, itself to be planned for. Over a day, we captured teachers moving quickly from work with challenging pupils to work with less challenging pupils, from teaching about the Roman Empire to teaching about the Second World War, from working with technology to deploying textbooks, and so on. Within the constraints of a manageable study we think that this gave us a picture of a variety of lessons.

The second element of data collection was drawn from two semi-structured interviews with the teacher we had observed. The first interview followed the day's observation closely, as soon as possible after the observed lessons. The interview data were in many ways the central data of our study. The lesson observations primarily provided data which could be developed and explored in interview. Interviewees were asked to begin by selecting two of the observed lessons they wished to discuss in detail. The interview then explored in considerable depth what the aims and objectives for these lessons had been and the extent to which they were achieved. The intention here was not to identify gaps between expressed and realized intentions, nor to reveal faults and errors in practice compared to aims and aspirations, but to understand the ways in which teachers translated their intentions into practice and the relative significance of different influences on this. The interviews provided opportunities for teachers to articulate in detail and in depth the basis of their practice which had been observed and the relationship to their perceptions of pupil needs, school context and expectations, curriculum specifications as well as wider understandings of the history curriculum. The second interviews, usually conducted several days later, then moved to a wider focus which explored the wider aspirations for history in the school curriculum in the study school. This interview explored curriculum organization and structure, the selection of content, materials and planned learning objectives and the major influences on these. It invited interviewees to consider overall aims for history teaching in their schools and to speculate on the future.

The final element of data collection was a documentary study of departmental and school policy documents. Largely under the influence of inspection, the quality, depth and range of departmental documentation in English secondary schools has increased hugely over the 1990s, and our requests for departmental handbooks and policy documents invariably produced extensive and heavy files. We were interested in a variety of material which could be drawn from the files. There was comparative factual information about the content of the history curriculum, the way different elements had been combined and the way performance within the department was monitored. At this level we were interested in the range and variety of learning opportunities presented to pupils, for example, by looking at the provision for fieldwork or the way schemes of work built in ICT and video material. The departmental documentation provided data on the overall aims and intentions for the history curriculum in our study schools, the way these aims were translated into aims for different study units and schemes of work, and the ways in which they planned for coherence and progression across the school.

Contextualizing practice in schools

Taken as whole, our data collection strategy allowed us to explore the relationship between aims and practice in the planned, articulated and observed work of a number of teachers. Fieldwork was conducted in eight comprehensive schools in England. The size of the study sample – eight schools – was determined in order to produce a study which was small enough to be manageable within the funding and time constraints, but sufficiently large to reflect a range of school sizes, types and settings. The study schools themselves were identified on a series of criteria, which, although not designed to construct a representative sample of English schools, were intended to ensure that a range of social, cultural and economic contexts of English schooling was represented. That said, some school types are not represented: the sample includes no selective or independent schools. We considered carefully the possibility of including independent schools and felt that the addition of an independent school would have been both interesting and potentially intriguing. However, we set out to explore the nature, pedagogy and aims of history teaching in a sample of the generality of English schools; the addition of a single independent school would have raised questions about its individual representativeness and we might have felt the need to add two or three such schools in order to test out the distinctiveness of independent schools, which would have unbalanced the sample. Furthermore, given that our eight schools themselves reflected a wide range of school types and settings, we were not persuaded that the study would have been markedly strengthened by the addition of independent schools. Figure 3.1 gives thumbnail portraits of the schools, drawn from the most recent Ofsted report for that school.

It was important that our schools reflected in some respects the range of characteristics of English schools. For this reason, the sample included schools with age ranges: 11–18, 11–16 and 13–19, as well as schools of different sizes. The average secondary school in England, on DfEE figures, educated just under 900 pupils in 2000 (DfEE 2000). Our sample included a range of school sizes (see Table 3.1). Although the study was not a study of school or departmental effectiveness, we wanted to work with schools which exhibited a

Table 3.1   The case study schools: summary data

	Age range	Number of pupils on roll	Pupils eligible for free school meals (%)	Pupils on SEN register (%)
Anderson	13–19	982	4	17.7
Brunel	11–18	987	8	15.5
Cromwell	11–18	1953	2	14.9
Darwin	11–18	970	6	20.3
Eliot	11–16	640	11	12.7
Foxe	11–18	950	5	9.2
Godwinson	11–18	1500	16	7.0
Hadrian	11–16	1086	55	18.5

Anderson School is an average sized urban upper school for 13–19-year-olds in a southern English city. Heavily oversubscribed, the school has an exceptionally wide range of levels of pupil attainment and a diverse catchment area, although the intake is skewed to the more able and socially advantaged. There is a very large sixth form. The school's population is mainly white but 9.3 per cent of pupils come from homes where English is an additional language. The history department is well established and well resourced. The head of history is Mark.

Brunel School is an average sized boys' comprehensive school for 11–18-year-olds in a small town in southern England which is currently experiencing significant population growth. The school catchment area includes estates of social housing, but the intake is fully comprehensive and pupils come from the full range of social and economic backgrounds. Very few pupils are from ethnic minority backgrounds. With the exception of the head of department, who has been in post for one year, all those who teach history have significant senior management responsibilities in the school. The head of history is Neil.

Cromwell School is a large mixed comprehensive for 11–18-year-olds in a small town in southern England. Although the school is relatively favoured in terms of economic and social factors there is a significant minority of pupils with special educational needs. The attainment of pupils covers the full range and if the large minority of pupils with special needs is discounted, there is a small upward skew in the attainment of pupils entering the school, although this does vary from year to year. There are very few pupils from ethnic minorities. The history department is part of a large humanities faculty and while all staff teach geography and R.E. as well as history to the lower school, there is a strong team of history specialists who work together in a well established and well resourced department, led by Peter, the head of department.

Darwin School is an above average sized mixed comprehensive for 11–18-year-olds situated in a rural area of southern England. The school caters for the full ability range: there are a good number of very able pupils and slightly more whose abilities are below or well below average. Very few pupils come from ethnic minority backgrounds. The percentage of pupils who live in high social class backgrounds is just below the national average and a considerable number come from relatively isolated and less advantaged backgrounds. About 40 pupils from travelling families attend the school. The head of history is Rachel.

Eliot School is a small semi-rural comprehensive school for 11–16-year-olds in the east of England, with an intake at both Year 7 (age 11+) and Year 8 (12+). The social context of the school is broadly average and attainment at entry matches the distribution of attainment nationally. There is a very small number of pupils for whom English is not their first language. The social context of the school is average. The history department is staffed by two full time staff members, including Keith, who is head of department, and one part time member of staff who trained as a geographer.

Foxe School is a school of average size for 11–18-year-olds, with about 140 pupils in the sixth form, in pleasant, rural surroundings in the north-west of England. The area from which the school draws its pupils is relatively advantaged. Almost all pupils speak English as their first language and are of European origin. On entry to the school pupils' attainment spans the full range of ability. The history department is small, with just two full time staff: Tom is head of department and Imogen is in her second year of teaching.

Figure 3.1: The case study schools

Godwinson School is a large, oversubscribed comprehensive school for 11–18-year-olds on the south-eastern edge of a Midlands city. The proportion of pupils reaching the expected level of attainment on entry varies from year to year but is above average overall. Both the proportion of pupils speaking English as an additional language and the proportion of pupils from ethnic minority backgrounds are above average. Most pupils come from families whose socio-economic circumstances are above the national average but about 10 per cent come from less favourable backgrounds. The history department is relatively large, with three full time staff led by Sarah, the head of history, and contributions from other staff. The department has played a significant role in LEA curriculum development projects.

Hadrian School is a comprehensive of average size for 11–16-year-olds in a south-western English city and draws its pupils from a variety of backgrounds. The majority, however, come from one of the most deprived local authority estates in the country. Attainment on entry is low and approximately 10 per cent of the pupils hold statements of special educational needs; and one third of the intake enter with a reading age three years below their chronological age. There are very few children from ethnic minorities. History is not currently offered post-16. The head of department is Lucy.

Figure 3.1: *continued*

wide range of socio-economic characteristics. The most widely used proxy for a school's socio-economic character remains the proportion of pupils eligible for free school meals; although a far from reliable guide, the available data on the study schools suggest that our sample includes a range of socio-economic characteristics (Table 3.1).

It was also important that the schools provided a range of attainment characteristics. Again, published data provide a thumbnail guide to the range of attainment characteristics in the schools. Table 3.2 presents two 'headline' performance characteristics on our study schools, relating to pupil performance at ages 16+ and 18+ in public examinations in the year 2000. The sample includes several high performing schools, a range of average performing schools and a school with apparently significant problems of under-achievement.

While the size, location and performance of the schools was important, of equal importance was the size, structure and organization of the history departments. The departmental structure of English secondary schools has been well entrenched for over 30 years, and the organizational structure of the contemporary comprehensive school typically owes a great deal to the formal structure of English grammar schools. This traditional structure assumes a head of department and, in history departments, one, two, or three close junior colleagues (Booth 1969). Recent emphases on school-based curriculum policy development and on the significance of departmental effectiveness in supporting whole school effectiveness, has tended to lay greater emphasis on the significance of departmental leadership (Harris 1999). However, at the

Table 3.2 The case study schools: examination and performance data

	GCSE results school (% scoring A*–C)	GCSE results history (% scoring A*–C)	Difference GCSE history vs GCSE School[1]	A level results school (average points score)	A level results history (average points score)
Anderson	62	86	+24	20.1	7.1
Brunel	43	43	0	17.2	6.5
Cromwell	59	65	+6	16.7	6.4
Darwin	49	68	+19	13.6	5.7
Eliot	62	71	+9	N/A	N/A
Foxe	61	65	+4	27.5	7.1
Godwinson	64	89	+1	19.0	6.3
Hadrian	24	22	–2	N/A	N/A

Note: (1) The data here suggests that in nearly every school the history department out-performed the school's average. In practice, the average figure for a school is heavily determined by core subjects (English, mathematics, science) for which all or nearly all pupils are entered for GCSE whereas history results are made up from those pupils who (a) opted for history and (b) completed the GCSE course.

same time, the coherence of the department has been weakened by a series of structural and contingent factors. The declining status of history as a subject in the 1990s, recruitment and retention difficulties in some schools, the increased emphasis on 'whole school' roles as a promotion route and the construction of faculties as management units all combined to weaken the grammar school model of the history department. We wanted to explore schools which presented different management structures for history. At the same time we wanted to ensure that the study departments were made up of a wide range of history teachers – those who had been teaching for a long time as well as recent entrants to the profession, with a variety of routes into the profession.

Hence our departments ranged in size from just two to seven members of staff. Their years of experience varied from one to 28. In one department, every history teacher other than the head of department had senior management responsibilities within the school. In another there were three members of the departmental staff whose main responsibilities were within the department. Some departmental members had a BEd degree, others an honours degree in history, others had a master's degree. One of our heads of department had been in post for one year, another for 24 years. This variety of departmental size, structure and organization was a strength of the study; these were departments at various stages of development, in schools experiencing the ordinary turbulence of English schools: staffing and curriculum changes, budgetary and timetable constraints, and uncertainties about pupil numbers.

Nonetheless, the sample was a small one. Eight schools, however varied, are unlikely to be wholly representative of a wider population. This book, therefore, is not offered simply as an account of a detailed research project. While we draw for examples and exemplification on our case study schools in the chapters which follow, we also explore a wider research framework for the study. We have already set out the research contexts in which we operated, and throughout the book we make cross-references to other research findings and research projects to set our findings from the case study schools into context. While the heart of the data comes from our observations of and discussions with teachers in the case study schools, we attempt throughout to show the wider lessons and conclusions we have drawn.

SECTION 2
Understanding history teachers

4   What do history teachers do in history classrooms?

Introduction

In 1969 Booth wrote,

> if pupils are to be believed, history lessons are often dull and seldom make demands; and the picture they present could and probably does apply to the majority of secondary schools. The lecturing, note making and note taking which seem to be such frequent occurrences rarely challenge the pupils or illuminate their understanding.
>
> (Booth 1969: 73)

Even though Booth's comments are based on the views of the pupils, the information he collected from the teachers themselves presents a similarly depressing picture of history lessons. Contrast that with our experience over 30 years later. We were rarely, if ever, bored, even when the lesson was yet again on Hitler's rise to power. We sat in richly diverse lessons, during which many of the pupils – even if not all – were evidently engaged in what they were doing, and were challenged to think and understand the history they were studying. Unlike Booth we did not seek the pupils' views on what was happening – there is no doubt it would have been good to have done so – but what we saw and heard in the lessons (and between us we have years of classroom observation experience) suggests to us that many of the students would share our view. What we observed, and were able to talk with the teachers about, was teaching and learning that has been transformed in the intervening 30 years since Booth's study.

In this chapter we concentrate on just three of our teachers and their lessons. Here, we look at what these teachers were intending to achieve through their teaching, how they tried to bring these intentions about, the sorts of activities they employed in the lessons and the sorts of issues that seemed to have impinged on their intentions. We have chosen three whose priorities are very different. For one, establishing the foundations of learning is crucial, for another teaching at Key Stage 3 can be 'real history' while at Key Stage 4 it is all about the exam and, for the last of our case studies, it is building historical understanding for all pupils that predominates. We conclude this chapter by bringing in our other teachers, considering briefly the ways in which they seem to be both similar and different to the three examined in detail.

Hadrian School

> The starting point has to be the particular group . . . I like to think that most of the things that I do within the classroom will encourage their own sense of self esteem and their own historical skills.
>
> (Lucy)

For Lucy, enabling the pupils to believe that they can learn and ensuring that they have confidence in themselves seemed to be central to her teaching. Her concern, in the context of a school whose social and economic circumstances are considerably below the national average (according to most recent Ofsted report) and where pupils' attainment on entry as measured by national tests puts them in the bottom 5 per cent nationally, was to establish the foundations of learning. For her, it was the affective dimension that took centre stage: until the pupils believed in themselves and saw the value of learning, little could be achieved.

Hence her intentions at Key Stage 3 were first and foremost to do with the pupils' confidence. In a Year 9 lesson, focusing on the key features of democracies and dictatorships, one of her objectives was to 'overcome their fear of these big words', 'to get them used to the words', so that they can 'work their way into it and begin to think I actually do know something about this'. This priority was expressed both in terms of the class as a whole and the individuals within it: 'It was quite interesting when Mark was clearly looking at me for my body language to see whether or not he might be right or wrong . . . he's a smart lad but has a complete lack of confidence in his own ability.' She wanted to ensure that they enjoyed their history lessons and felt able to participate. Similarly with a Year 8 group studying Richard Arkwright, she wanted them to have fun with the activities and used her questioning, for example, to ensure that 'the students can participate in the lesson'. Their interest in what they were doing was important to her – especially given the topic – and that they remained on task most of the time. She wanted to build on their previous successes – 'a bit of security, I suppose' – so that they could continue to achieve and make progress. While these sorts of intentions or goals predominated, they were not the only ones. Literacy and oracy skills were also important. For Year 9 it was familiarity with important vocabulary, with words that 'are not used very widely' but which, once understood through their history lessons, 'they'll be quite pleased when they ask their parent, granny, next door neighbour and they may not know what these terms are and they do'. With Year 8 the goal was writing skills: extending what they had done in the past so that they could produce an 'in depth piece, which includes evidence to support what they say about Arkwright'. For all her lessons 'literacy is a huge factor'. What of her intentions specifically to do with historical understanding? They were there, but did not seem to be the priority. She wanted Year 8 to understand Arkwright's successes, and to do so in the context of changes between 1750 and 1900. For Year 9 the intention was that they should develop some basic understanding of dictatorship and democracy, ideas that were central to the whole Year 9 course. It was interesting that in talking about her lessons and about the goals or objectives for them Lucy began by stating that these aspirations related to historical understanding, and yet as she talked more about what she was hoping to achieve in the lesson they seemed to recede. While historical understanding was the ultimate goal, in these lessons, other priorities had to come first.

How then did she seek to achieve her intentions? What sorts of tasks and activities did she use? The central task in the Arkwright lesson was a game about being a successful entrepreneur, from Britain 1750–1900 *Special Needs Support Materials* (Shepherd and Brown 1996: 47–52). The pupils' aim – in a simple game of chance – was, initially, to make as much money as possible. Once the game had been played the pupils used cards from the game to establish a chronology of Arkwright's successes and finally to assess the significance of particular factors – such as investment capital and advertising – in his successes. While the information and ideas built into the game were obviously important to Lucy – and especially that there were specific reasons for Arkwright's success – it was her concern that the pupils should enjoy what they were doing through a 'fun activity' that predominated. It contributed to an active lesson which interested the pupils: 'the activity drew them into it'. The game and its related tasks were followed by pupils reading aloud sources about Arkwright (Shepherd and Brown 1996: 54) and considering, as a whole class, if they showed approval or disapproval for the entrepreneur. The final part of the lesson was devoted to setting up the written task – an obituary of Arkwright – to be completed with the aid of a writing frame. Throughout the lesson, the pupils' participation was also secured by Lucy's questioning. At the beginning of the lesson it served to help the pupils remember what they already knew about this period, later in the lesson it sought to draw out what they had been learning from the game, and throughout 'it's the way students can participate'. Her questioning also enabled her to check the pupils' understanding, to see if they were 'tapping into the right direction I want the lesson to go'. Lucy enjoyed this lesson and knew that her intentions that the pupils were involved and on task were achieved: 'it was a good building block to move on with'.

The Year 9 lesson also involved an activity using the Schools History Project (SHP) support materials, here from the *Twentieth Century World* book (Shephard and Moore 1997: 96–9), but this time there was an extensive question and answer session preceding it, lasting over 15 minutes, in which Lucy sought to establish the sorts of knowledge and understanding the pupils might already have of the words 'dictatorship' and 'democracy'. Through probing their awareness of the current political systems in this country, it became apparent that the pupils knew very little about politics and she herself was 'surprised that they weren't more aware of the different political parties'. She hoped that the pupils would begin to recognize Britain today as a democracy and that key characteristics of this are the existence of a range of political parties, open elections and the right to express one's opinion. Although pupil understanding of these issues was very variable she moved the lesson onto the SHP activity with the pupils matching statements about democracy and dictatorship to cartoons illustrating these features. The shift to this activity was as much about the pupils' concentration and engagement as their understanding: 'it's a change of activity . . . It's time to move in a different direction but not lose the thread . . . it lightens the lesson . . . it's a difficult topic: cutting and glueing, why not?' The lesson concluded with a brief plenary, with feedback from the pupils about examples of key features. Lucy was a little disappointed by this lesson. She was pleased with the initial discussion and thought they would be able to build on that in future lessons but they didn't get as far as she had hoped in matching up the cards: 'I think the end could have been stronger . . . I wasn't able to conclude it as much or make the points as much as I wanted.'

Lucy knew exactly what it was she wanted to achieve in these lessons and had carefully chosen the activities that she would use to bring about these aspirations. In making these choices a range of differing factors were significant in her thinking. Most apparent was her knowledge of her pupils. She wanted to start from where they were, in terms of their low levels of confidence, their existing knowledge and the skills they already had. For both lessons she knew that 'there's a lot that they aren't aware of and I'm aware of that' and she asked herself the question, 'What is their starting point?' She was acutely aware of behaviour issues and that many of the pupils found it hard to concentrate and remain settled. The pupils needed structure, a range of varied activities and pace in their lessons. Interestingly though, 'good behaviour' was not, in itself, one of her goals. Her goal was that these pupils should learn how to learn and begin to grapple with the ideas and substance of history. Behaviour management was a means to a much more important end. To achieve these ends another significant factor was evidently what had gone before and what would come next. The demands of particular exercises in terms of generic skills like literacy and the need for appropriate sequencing within the curriculum and within each lesson were both important for Lucy. Each lesson was linked to others so that Lucy operated with an overview of what would be needed at each stage if the pupils were to make the progress she hoped for: she often talked in terms of 'setting pupils up' for future learning and 'going back and revisiting'. Ideas about progression were deeply embedded in her practice. So too was her recognition of the challenges that history itself presents: history is difficult. But, as with the other factors, it seemed that none of these were negative constraints. Instead they were issues that affected what she sought to do and how she set about that. They were characteristics of what she was trying to teach and who she was trying to teach that to, but they did not stand in her way.

She wanted her 'pupils to achieve, to have an interest and enthusiasm for the subject, to want to be in the classroom, to want to learn . . . To see that history is something they can join in with, they can participate in'.

Brunel School

> It comes up commonly in the exams – that's the only reason . . . this topic can be used to deliver a certain historical experience and reinforce why history is important.
>
> (Neil)

What needs to be achieved and what can be achieved was, for Neil, profoundly affected by the curriculum and statutory requirements. His concerns differed markedly depending on the key stage at which he was teaching. At Key Stage 4, what were seen as the requirements of the examination dominated. The need for pupils to acquire and then regurgitate factual information took precedence to the extent that Neil felt himself not to be teaching history at all – he was teaching to an exam. In contrast, history at Key Stage 3 could be history, with opportunities for enquiry, investigation, debate, depth and overview. An important additional emphasis across the key stages was literacy: a whole school priority. On entry to this all boys school, standards of literacy are low and history, along with other departments, is seeking to address this. This is a genuinely comprehensive school, with an intake that comes from the full range of social and economic backgrounds. Levels of achievement both within the school as a whole and in history are in line with national average comparisons.

The stark differences in emphasis played themselves out in the lessons observed. Neil's central intention in the Year 10 lesson, focusing on why Gorbachev tried to change the Soviet Union, was 'to get the content across'. There were two key ideas that he wanted the boys to both understand and remember: glasnost and perestroika. Why those? 'Because they come up commonly in the exam, that's the only reason . . . they're key questions in past exam papers.' He wanted them to understand these ideas and to 'build connections and bridges in their minds' but 'if the syllabus doesn't have it I don't waste time covering it'. Ensuring that they were likely to remember what they had learned required constant reinforcement, so the lesson was peppered with occasions for recap and consolidation: 'they need constant reminders of the key terms'. The way that the examination requires the boys to demonstrate their knowledge was an equally important goal. They have to be able to write it down in an essay form and hence he used a range of strategies to help them learn how to organize the information appropriately. Without this 'their presentation is poor – they just write a block – there's no way they can order it for themselves'. The Year 9 lesson, with a lower band group who are 'always a battle', was directed by what Neil felt was important about the history and its value for the boys. The key question for the lesson was 'Who was Adolf Hitler and how did he come to power in Germany?' Here Neil's intention was that the pupils should understand that 'certain things had to happen for Hitler to come to power'. He wanted them to consider why people were attracted to Hitler and why people voted for him. He linked this to challenging contemporary stereotypes about the Germans, especially in relation to sport and the boys' inevitable interest in football. In this lesson, Neil had felt able to chose his own priorities – 'it's my personal approach' – and does not feel constrained by the syllabus. He could make the history what he wanted it to be and shape his lessons around this.

Although Neil's intentions at GCSE were shaped by external forces, he nonetheless felt able to achieve them in this lesson. He used a range of varying activities to ensure that the boys collected and ordered factual information about the problems Gorbachev faced and the solutions he proposed. After a brief recap through whole class questioning, the boys were moved into groups to investigate a particular problem faced by Gorbachev (industry, agriculture, foreign policy) or a particular policy line he pursued (perestroika and glasnost). Each group had a range of resources to draw on, mostly drawn from their textbook (Walsh 1996: 324), and their task was to research their topic independently, with Neil helping the groups in turn. These investigations were brought together by the creation, on the board, of a spider diagram, created through feedback from the groups and manipulated by Neil so that it contained the key information that he required. The pupils recorded this in their books and when they finished they read – silently – a short section from the textbook. The lesson concluded with repeated questioning of individuals about the meanings of the terms 'glasnost' and 'perestroika'. Neil was happy with this lesson and although he didn't get through quite as much as he had wanted he felt that 'the majority have gone away knowing what glasnost and perestroika are and that at least half of them would be able to expand on that a little bit more'. In contrast, Neil's intentions for Year 9, while of his own choice, were somewhat thwarted in the lesson 'because classroom management became more of an issue than the history at the end'. The lesson involved a series of activities chosen to take the boys through conditions in Germany in the 1920s, Hitler's ideas and the events of the early 1930s. Each of the three main activities was based on a textbook worksheet. The first, focusing on what Germany was like in the 1920s, required some individual reading of texts and scrutiny of two photographs illustrating hyperinflation in order to identify in writing three things that made life hard for German people. A brief feedback on this was then followed by a sheet that set out Hitler's beliefs (in the form of thought bubbles emanating from a drawing of Hitler's head) and required these to be matched and placed in given categories such as the Treaty of Versailles, his opponents, the economy and parliament and the government. Again, there was brief feedback before the penultimate activity. This involved pairs of pupils sorting a series of cartoons, representing events from the 1920s and early 1930s, into chronological order, with the requirement to think about why one event may have led to another. Neil led a plenary from this in which he sought to establish a series of linked events in which each had significant consequences for what came next. The lesson concluded with a 'filling in the blanks' written exercise drawing on the information from the chronology task. For Neil, the first two activities – on Germany in the 1920s and Hitler's ideas – achieved what he wanted: 'I'm reasonably happy that the majority of them would have understood because we had a coming together and reinforcing of all these links. At that point I was quite happy.' But he knew that by the second half of the lesson 'there were fires going off here and there', time and concentration were being lost and hence he was not able to make all the links he had intended, especially in terms of economic problems and Hitler's rise to power. Ultimately, he felt that 'I don't necessarily feel the majority could give a reason why Hitler came to power.'

Two contrasting lessons. In one, with goals essentially determined by external considerations, Neil felt he was able to achieve what he had set out to do. In the other, where he set his own agenda, he felt he had only limited success. What sorts of issues seemed to have been significant in his thinking and practice? For Year 10 it was clear that the over-riding considerations were the examination syllabus and the examining requirements. Those, coupled with his knowledge of the boys and what they would find hard (like sorting information, remembering it and expressing it in writing), were the key factors. Although with Year 10 he took account of the fact that with this particular group he could not leave them for too long on any one task, the behaviour of the pupils did not seem to be a major consideration. In contrast, with Year 9 this was clearly a significant factor in trying to implement his plan. In thinking about what he wanted to achieve in the lesson it seemed that he was especially concerned that the boys understood certain historical ideas and especially the notion of cause and consequence. But in the lesson itself 'the mood they're in, it destroys the flow and pace' and a key consequence of this is that time is lost: 'everything takes longer than expected'. To some degree he anticipated this as 'it's always the same and I try to break it up and have maybe six options for the lesson, but maybe expect to get through only four'. One might have anticipated that in the lesson where the teacher felt able to choose his own goals he would have more success in achieving them, especially given his knowledge of the class and the challenges they were likely to present. It might be that, precisely because of his commitment to the historical goals, his recognition of how the class was likely to respond got a little lost until the reality presented itself, and forcibly too. Another explanation may be that, as yet, Neil does not have as rich a repertoire, as, for example, Lucy, of the sorts of tasks and activities that he might use to achieve his goals. He is only in his second year of teaching, and while head of department, he is inevitably short of experience. To link successfully knowledge of the pupils with intentions for lessons requires that a teacher be able to make choices from a great fund of ideas about what might be appropriate for particular classes and individuals and specific sorts of goals. Such funds take years of investment to accumulate. For Neil, the issues that seemed to impinge on his practice did seem like constraints; he experienced the syllabus requirements as such, and the behavioural challenges presented by Year 9 undoubtedly prevented him from achieving all that he wanted.

Anderson School

> I tell every Y9 group everyone can do it . . . You can have a kind of level of historical understanding that pervades everything . . . and that's a bridge in.
>
> (Mark)

Mark teaches in Anderson School, a school that recruits from the full spectrum of ability and a wide social mix, although its intake, according to Ofsted, is skewed towards the more able and the socially advantaged. The school's results, as we have seen, are well above the national average and in history in 2000, 86 per cent achieved A*–C at GCSE. It is in this context that Mark seeks to build historical understanding in his teaching of history. Historical under-standing is seen in terms of both the substantive and procedural knowledge of the discipline and Mark firmly believes that such understanding can be made accessible to all. Pupils in the final years of Key Stages 3 and 4 can have access to the complex discipline of history, a discipline mediated for them by Mark.

At both Key Stage 3 and Key Stage 4, it was building specific types of historical knowledge and understanding that dominated Mark's intentions in the lessons observed. The Key Stage 3 lesson focused on the German invasion of the Soviet Union during the Second World War. Goals for this lesson operated at a number of levels. An overarching goal was that pupils develop an overview of key events or turning points in the war and, within this overview, that they understood why Hitler chose to attack the Soviet Union and why the invasion failed. The teacher's intentions were equally clear for each section of the lesson and he deliberately set the lesson up so that pupils themselves would ask the question about why Hitler attacked – he did not pose the question for them. He then wanted them to recognize that there were a range of linked reasons. He wanted 'everybody to get an understanding of at least a range of reasons why this happened', recognizing that some were 'complex and ideological, while others are very standard to do with oil and grain' and the pupils would vary in what they understood. As to the reasons for failure, again the intention was that the question be generated by the pupils rather than the teacher, and the final section of the lesson was guided by this intention. Closely linked to these detailed intentions about the historical understanding to be generated was the intention that it be accessible to all, but in ways which were differentiated for different pupils. At the outset of the lesson he wanted to draw the pupils in 'not just go blustering in saying right, we've got an invasion of Russia or it would have been "What's this all about?" They actually need to get into the mindset'. Once they had all got 'into the mindset', he had different goals for different pupils: 'I'm thinking certainly him or her would be able to get all those, and so and so might not be able to do all that but they will be able to get this idea'. He was less concerned about exactly what they would each understand about the reasons for attack and defeat than he was that all would know that there were a range of reasons and within the range they had understood, would be able to prioritize them in order of importance.

These linked goals – of making history accessible and hence building historical understanding – were also those that characterized and similarly permeated the Year 10 lesson. The particular focus here was factors related to Hitler's rise to power and specifically the role of propaganda in this. But the lesson did not stand alone: it was one of a series of lessons on why Hitler came to power, and the purpose of looking at propaganda was 'beginning to help them to empathise with what the German people were faced with'. Again, each part of the lesson was, in its own way, directed towards this so that through detailed analysis of different forms of propaganda, and a consideration of the context in which they were deployed, the pupils would come to recognize their skill and effectiveness and hence the sorts of impact they would have had on the German population. Throughout he wanted the pupils to think, and used resources he knew would promote this. He was clear on the core ideas or pieces of information that all must grasp : 'everyone needs to get that he was a good speaker, the very clear symbol in his swastika, that he aimed at different types of people'. But he also anticipated that others would be able to go further to recognize that 'he was a very good speaker partly because he was reflective and that he worked hard at audience manipulation and that was part of the Nazi package of the management of a crowd'. But while he intended that some would develop higher levels of understanding, he would not risk 'confusing things for others' and hence a contribution to class feedback, for example, might have been 'tweaked' so it could be included but if that wasn't possible it would not be included in any summary. He had a 'benchmark that everybody needs to get' and he intended to ensure that they all achieved that.

What, then, did Mark do to achieve his remarkably clear and coherent intentions? What sorts of tasks and activities were employed in the lessons? Both lessons involved a whole series of varied, relatively small, linked tasks with strong teacher direction and leadership throughout. The Year 9 lesson began with teacher questioning designed to establish the 'mindset' Mark wanted. Through the pupils' responses, he traced the early events of the war from its outbreak in 1939 through to 1940, mentioning Dunkirk, the Battle of Britain and the Blitz en route. He established with them that by the end of 1940, Britain stood alone in Europe, but that this was all to change when Hitler turned his attention to the east, despite the existence of the Nazi–Soviet pact. At this point, two cartoons were introduced, both from the *Peace and War* textbook (Shephard *et al.* 1993: 130, 138) and questioning about the content of these contemporary documents established that the alliance was very unstable and that, in 1940, Hitler attacked Russia. A brief section of video, showing action on the Eastern Front, was shown and stopped at the point when the commentary stated that this was the biggest mistake that Hitler had made. Pupils were then directed to a school produced resource containing a range of primary and secondary sources on the reasons for the invasion and they worked individually to look for these reasons. Feedback from this, again through whole class question and answer, raised economic and military issues and an excursion – unintended by Mark – into differences in ideology between Nazism and communism. Having established a range of reasons for the attack, another, uninterrupted, piece of video was used to show how initially successful the invasion was for the Germans. The teacher then posed the question: 'Why did it all go disastrously wrong?' The pupils were directed back to their sheets to find at least ten reasons and worked on this until the end of the lesson with the intention that feedback from this activity would be the starting point for the next lesson.

The mix of whole class questioning, relatively short tasks and frequent feedback was also evident in the Year 10 lesson. The lesson began with question and answer, in which Mark first asked 'What is propaganda?' and having received an answer that it was information designed to make people think in certain ways, went on to establish what sorts of things would make effective propaganda. After ten minutes of this whole class activity an overhead transparency showing three examples of Nazi propaganda was introduced. Each of the pupils had a copy of this sheet. The first example was a photograph of a mass rally and, through question and answer, Mark led the pupils to annotate the photograph with labels indicating the way the occasion worked as a form of propaganda – for example, a mass crowd organized in rows, big clear symbols like the swastika flags, and so on. The second was an election poster showing a family group and with the caption 'Women! Millions of men out of work. Millions of children without a future. Save our German families. Vote for Adolf Hitler!' Here, the emphasis in the question and answer session was on establishing the group targeted by the poster and the idea of the existence of a problem for which the Nazis had a solution. The third example examined and annotated in this way was a written source of impressions of hearing Hitler speak and so the emphasis here was on Hitler's own speeches and their potential power. Throughout this section of the lesson, the pupils were annotating their own copies of these examples of Nazi propaganda. Following this, the pupils were shown an example of 'propaganda in action' – a video clip showing Hitler speaking at a mass rally – and this was followed by a discussion of how Hitler had spoken and behaved. The final section of the lesson was introduced by Mark saying that the propaganda would not have been effective if there hadn't been problems in Germany to be solved. Pupils were given a sheet entitled 'How did the Depression help the Nazis?' This contained a number of primary and secondary sources suggesting the ways in which the depression impacted on several different groups in society such as the unemployed, businessmen, young people, farmers and so on. Individually pupils worked on the impact of the Depression on these groups until the end of the lesson. In both lessons Mark felt that he had been able to achieve what he wanted. As he said,

> both lessons you've seen today have tended to be very similar in that what I've been doing is to work through quite a lot of material and they've been working individually, and then coming back, and lots of question and answering. I would anticipate from the number who got involved and asked questions and answered questions, from what was going down in their books, yes – they've pretty much got the ideas I wanted.

A number of factors seemed to impinge on Mark's thinking and practice. A central issue was clearly the nature and complexity of the subject matter. He saw the subject both in terms of its substantive content (why Hitler came to power, why he invaded the Soviet Union) and its procedural or organizing concepts (the concept of causation, the nature of historical evidence) and these were closely united in his thinking and teaching. He was very clear about the particular ideas that he wanted pupils to understand and he recognized which ideas were more complex than others and hence would not be accessible to all. He was sure of when he wanted specific information and when he was happy with pupils understanding in more general terms. When he led the question and answer session, a central feature of his lessons, he knew what he wanted – 'I've got set things which I know I want them to write down' – but he was also alert to what the pupils might raise: 'I try to be a little bit responsive.' He knew what 'might take them down a wrong avenue, or it's just too much'. Another closely linked issue was curriculum and lesson sequencing. Each lesson was seen as one of a series, each with its own part to play in developing the understanding he wanted. Within each lesson, each part of it had a specific role and in every case this was to contribute to the building of historical understanding. As he had a strong sense of what the pupils would be able to achieve in a given time and with a given resource or activity, he 'knows how it's going to go down and what the best way of doing it is'. It was evident that he has built up a bank of resources and ideas for activities that he knew would enable him to achieve his goals, and by 'looking at the group, looking at what the situation is, what time of day, what I've done before' he was able to bridge the potential gap between the discipline of history and his pupils.

Conclusion

Lucy, Neil and Mark have enabled us to access three very different classroom environments. While there is much that they share – perhaps most notably their concern to do their best by their pupils – they differ in important ways. Their intentions vary, from the dominance of the affective domain for Lucy, to the priority accorded to sophisticated historical understanding by Mark. All deliberately seek to engage their learners but what this means for each differs. For Neil and especially Lucy, their intentions go way beyond the historical: the needs of their pupils, in the contexts within which they teach, demand this of them. While they seek to achieve their goals in differing ways, for all three there is a substantial mix of both independent activity by the pupils and teacher-led work. Questioning is critically important to each teacher; it is what drives Mark's lessons forward, it is one of the means for Lucy to engage and reassure her pupils, it offers the possibility of the links and connections that Neil aspires to create for the pupils. In each classroom the independent activities make a range of demands on the pupils. In Lucy's lessons, decision making, sorting, prioritizing and having fun are all apparent. The boys with whom Neil works are required to make selections from information, to order this information and to think about sequence. In Mark's classroom, the pupils are challenged to think in detail about why things happened and to develop skills of analysis and synthesis. Each teacher is evidently affected by a wide range of factors in their thinking and their practice – from the behavioural challenges that some pupils present, to the demands of an examination, to their own particular view of what is important in history. For our two most experienced teachers – Lucy and Mark – these factors seem to operate simply as conditions of which they take account; they do not limit what they feel able to achieve. For Neil, there is much more of a sense of feeling constrained and being unable, as yet, to balance what seem to be the competing demands of what he wants to achieve and the ways in which the class may behave. What of our other teachers? In what ways are they similar or different to these three?

In terms of their intentions, a similar range was found among the others. Goals associated with various types of historical understanding were evident for all. Sometimes these were expressed in terms of the substantive content: to understand the debates surrounding the introduction of the National Health Service or to understand why the Good Friday Agreement was possible, for example. At other times, they were expressed in terms of procedural concepts: for the pupils, through their study of castles, to learn about chronology and change over time or, in relation to the assassination of Kennedy, to develop skills in handling historical evidence. Frequently, these emphases were inter-linked so that, for example, the point of developing evidential skills in the Kennedy lesson was to enable the pupils to be able to understand more fully why one of the theories about Kennedy's assassination could implicate the security services. All, in different ways, sought to engage their pupils. There was rarely the assumption that pupils would automatically be interested or intrigued; through the ways in which they structured the lessons, through the activities they used, through the ways they used themselves in the lessons, these teachers all sought to motivate, interest and involve the pupils and keep them on task throughout their lessons. Several of the teachers had literacy development as an important goal, either in terms of pupils beginning to learn what it means to construct an argument or in learning about the range of ways this needs to be expressed in the written form. For these teachers, developing literacy meant developing writing. Although pupils were encouraged to con-tribute orally and in a variety of ways in all our lessons, the intention with the talk was that it should play a role in developing the pupils' understanding or their sense of engagement with what they were doing. It was not about, for example, developing pupils' capacity to present an argument in oral form. For two of our teachers their intentions were explicitly related to the moral dimension. Hence a lesson on the Holocaust was deliberately focused on encouraging the pupils to see it in the context of moral judgements while a lesson on the black peoples of the Americas was targeted at the development of anti-racist attitudes.

In seeking to bring about their intentions, the teachers employed a wide range of strategies. For all of them, questioning was a central feature of their lessons. It had a wide range of different purposes: to engage the learners, to reassure them, to move lessons on and increase the pace, to recap on knowledge previously acquired, to enable the teacher to discover what the pupils already knew and understood or the ways in which their understanding was developing, to encourage the pupils to think and develop that thinking, to enable them to report to their classmates what they had discovered, to enable the teacher to impart information, to make links and connections for the pupils or to encourage them to do so. Questioning came at the start of the lessons, between activities and as a means of concluding the lesson. The activities that engaged the pupils involved them working on their own, in pairs and in groups. They ranged from the relatively straightforward writing of answers, to comprehension questions, to the creation of a form of living graph in which pupils plotted events leading up to the Good Friday Agreement against an axis of peace, to tension and armed conflict. Pupils worked in pairs to construct a conversation between two doctors, one for and the other against the introduction of the National Health Service. They worked in groups investigating changes in Chepstow Castle over time. As whole classes they looked at videos, in one lesson analysing the differing interpretations of Robin Hood presented by different movies, in another watching uninterrupted to learn about what actually happened during the Final Solution. In the lesson on Kennedy's assassination, pupils worked with diverse forms of evidence: a model, a shirt, a video, as well as written documents. In many of the lessons textbooks and the accompanying teachers' guides were an important resource for both teachers and pupils. They acted as sources of information and as sources of evidence about the past. Some of their activities were central features of lessons but they were used in a highly diverse manner by our teachers and their use was interspersed by other tasks and resources. Pupils adopted the roles of individuals in the past, they reported to the class through various types of presentation, they contributed to feedback and brainstorms, they answered and asked questions. Simultaneously, teachers worked with the class as a whole and the individuals within it. They targeted questions and tasks at individuals and at groups, they supported both as they worked individually and collectively. They managed time, space, pupils, resources and ideas.

For all the teachers, their actions and their thinking were affected by diverse factors. Their knowledge of their pupils, their interests, capabilities and needs governed much that they did, as did their historical goals and intentions. What they knew about how pupils learn and how particular historical understandings can be achieved had a profound effect on how they sequenced the curriculum and individual lessons within it. Their knowledge of different resources and strategies enabled them to make selections to bridge the gap between their learners and their aspirations for them. In different contexts different emphases emerged. The work on castles was especially affected by the teacher's knowledge of her pupils' preferences, whereas the work on analysing the video on Robin Hood was affected by the teacher's view that film and media sources are important sources of information for young people. Choices about the study of both Northern Ireland and the Holocaust were bound up with the teacher's commitment to the relevance of history to pupils' everyday lives. The need to ensure pupils have a reason for wanting to contribute and investigate further was pre-eminent in the lesson on Kennedy and the black peoples of the Americas. The importance of overview – of both pupils' learning and the history itself – was apparent for all the teachers, and its absence was specifically identified as a constraint by one of the least experienced teachers.

What emerges from these classrooms is a picture that is very different from that portrayed by Booth (1969). The principal similarity would seem to be the importance of the spoken word. But the resonance ends there. Booth's teachers 'made it clear that the spoken word is their main classroom method – that the children must be told' (1969: 63). Booth goes on to comment that

> the crucial point is the manner and the purpose of the telling. Does it involve and illuminate understanding? Or does it merely deaden so that the words slide over the pupils? The impression given in the interviews was that too often pupils feel that they are being talked at rather than with.
>
> (Booth 1969: 63)

The evidence of our classrooms is that the spoken word is used to involve and illuminate understanding. Teachers did just 'tell', but they also used videos, textbooks, school produced resources and the pupils themselves to do the telling. When the teacher was the source of information, the telling was done in an interactive way, with frequent questioning of the pupils and the use of other resources to support it. Of course we too observed the 'disciplinary difficulties' (Booth 1969: 64) that, as Booth comments, can jeopardize the interaction between teacher and pupils achieved through talk. But the response of our teachers to this was to seek alternative ways of engaging the pupils, through interesting activities like games or puzzling tasks that required thinking. Booth bemoans that lack of variety and the lack of challenge and stimulation which characterized history lessons. Our lessons were replete with both.

5 What do history teachers know?

It is just after Mark's lesson with Year 10 focusing on why Hitler came to power and in particular, the role of propaganda in this. Mark is discussing his lesson and specifically his use of three particular examples: a photograph of a mass rally, a written source of impressions of hearing Hitler speak and an election poster showing a family group, with the caption 'Women! Millions of men out of work. Millions of children without a future. Save our German families. Vote for Adolf Hitler!'

Can you remember why you originally chose the three particular sources?

Probably because I nicked them off Simon (another member of the department). But I think the real reason was because they show a range of different features: the mass meeting, the oral evidence, and also the poster source. A range of things. They make some of the points very nicely which the kids had already got from the previous work about it, so in other words they provide appropriate examples in action of the things that they've already learnt that the Nazis viewed as significant. And also, when it's put with the video, they actually provide quite a nice set of materials. Once they've looked at that and looked at the video as well, hopefully it begins to mean something, what this was really all about.

And is there any particular reason why you do that annotating?

I just think it's quite a good way of making them think, and about this in action. It's a better way of getting them to draw things out of it. Again it's something which I think at times in the past I've just got them to do in groups, but actually it's quite a brief little activity so it doesn't really demand that so much. I just think again it's a quite nice diagrammatical way of showing that, and then they can stick it in their books, and they've got some nice things they can actually refer to.

Mark didn't just happen to think this was a nice activity to use with Year 9 – his rationales for choosing the three propaganda examples reveal a great deal about the richness of his thinking and how all sorts of knowledge – about history, about his pupils, about what will help them to learn – are embedded within his experience. He has knowledge of the history and what it is about propaganda that he wants the pupils to understand: 'they show a range of different features: the mass meeting, the oral evidence, and also the poster source. A range of things . . . appropriate examples in action'. He shows his knowledge of resources and activities which will help him to lead the pupils to develop the understandings that he wants: 'They make some of the points very nicely', 'when it's put with the video, they actually provide quite a nice set of materials', 'it's quite a good way of making them think', 'it's a quite nice diagrammatical way of showing that'. His language hints at his knowledge of the pupils, of what will be 'a good way of making them think', but this emerges more clearly in the next stage of the interview:

And did you know exactly what labels you wanted to get?

Yes, pretty much. Although, as I said, the symbols and the women, the focus on the target group and so on, but every year somebody will pick up something, somebody said about the critical faculty part, which again I don't normally annotate, but I thought that was quite a nice idea to bring in, so I try and be a little bit responsive if they bring in anything different, but I've got to set things which I know I want them to write down.

How do you decide not to put something in?

That's a really good question, actually. Probably because I can't spell it. That's usually a big thing. I'm just thinking. I'll only not put it up if I think it's actually going to make things more confusing for everybody else. So if somebody says something which is either too complex or rather half understood, I'll try and tweak it so that it either means something so we can put it up, or not, if you see what I mean.

I think it was Jim who raised stuff to do with the Whitman source and idea of German manhood? And you didn't put that up. Was that elaborating more than. . .?

I think probably that's right. Yes. It was a very subtle, complex idea which actually for the purpose of this might have been a little bit too much for some people. I think that's the point, it's when it would take them down the wrong avenue, or it's just too much.

Here he shows his knowledge about what will help and what will serve to confuse learning for his pupils; he makes judgements as the lesson progresses about which of the ideas they can cope with and which need to be acknowledged but not emphasized.

What we seek to do in this chapter is to dig deeper behind the teachers' intentions, the activities they used and the factors that impinge on their teaching – all illustrated in Chapter 4 – to see if we can uncover what it is that underpins their skilled endeavours. Trying to find an appropriate way of doing this has not been easy, as – like Mark, albeit in a very different context – we were juggling with all sorts of concerns. We wanted to build on other research that has been done on teachers and teaching; we wanted to ensure that we had a chance to capture the fact that we were working with teachers of history, rather than in another subject and we wanted to be faithful to our teachers and what they actually said to us – we did not want to distort their voices by looking at what they said only through lenses provided by others. We also wanted to make sure that we could find a way of talking about them that would resonate for all our teachers and not just one or two, and we wanted to do all this in terms that did not rely on obscure concepts that might be favoured by social scientists but would be barely recognizable to practitioners.

We came up with a relatively simple way of looking at what our teachers told us, influenced by the literature on teacher knowledge which asks 'What do teachers know in order to do the things they do? What sorts of knowledge seem to be embedded in their thinking and their practice?' There have been many studies of this, representing a variety of ways of either trying to make sense of the knowledge that teachers actually possess or presenting the knowledge that someone else thinks they should have (see, for example, Carter 1990, Feiman-Nemser and Remillard 1995; Verloop *et al.* 2001). We have not attempted to explore some of the fine distinctions made by other researchers about, for example, knowledge in use or propositional types of knowledge, nor differences between, say, practical and personal knowledge. Instead we have taken a stance that was prompted by an extensive review of our data, and which is – as it turned out – supported by other studies. Our intention was not to generate knowledge *for* teachers (Fenstermacher 1994) but knowledge *of* teachers. Hence we look at three major types of teacher knowledge that emerged from what they said to us: their knowledge about their subject, their knowledge about their pupils and their knowledge of the sorts of resources and activities that they could use to bring about their goals in their lessons. Such a classification or typology of teachers' knowledge resonates with other studies, although it is simpler than many. The inclusion of the teachers' knowledge about subject was not assumed. Although we were interested in the concept of pedagogical content knowledge first developed by Shulman (1986), we were conscious too of its limitations (see, for example, Pendry 1994;

Bullough 2001; Van Driel *et al.* 2001). Much of that research works from the assumption that teachers ought to be concerned with their subject and hence are framed in terms that have often led to deficit models of teachers' expertise. However, although we did not make the same assumptions, it was very evident that this was an important type of knowledge for all but one of our teachers and very recent work in this field (Grossman 2002) helped us to consider it in terms of questions to be asked rather than answers given. As we asked the questions of our data, it was evident that the teachers had much to say about subject knowledge and hence it was included in our typification. Our use of the term 'teacher knowledge' is, like that of Verloop *et al.* (2001), one that encompasses teachers' beliefs. As they say, 'in the mind of the teacher components of knowledge, beliefs and intuitions are inextricably intertwined' (p. 446).

As we have now moved from the 'little stories' of the individual teachers and their lessons towards a 'bigger picture' of history teachers' expertise, we have left their individual names behind. What they told us and their words remain central, but now we explore this detail in terms that might apply to many teachers.

What sorts of knowledge about school history do these teachers seem to hold?

All of the teachers talked of both the substantive and procedural dimensions of history. This distinction has been described by Lee and Ashby (2001) thus:

> substantive history is the content of history, what history is 'about' . . . procedural ideas about history . . . concepts like historical evidence, explanation, change are ideas that provide our understanding of history as a discipline or form of knowledge. They are not what history is 'about' but they shape the way we go about doing history.

Each teacher made reference to the substance, or content, that they wanted their pupils to understand, but this was seen through the lens of one or more procedural concepts. Hence the lesson on the introduction of the National Health Service was, for this teacher, both about the specific debates and events (in some detail) that led to its inception but was also about the pupils' understanding that it is a representation of change over time: 'I wanted to build for them to get a feeling of change over time.' The idea of change over time was also reflected in the lesson on castles. Here, it was so strong that for the teacher 'it isn't really castles at all, it's getting the kids to appreciate that things are not going to stay the same across five hundred years'. While one teacher talked of the importance of looking at Arkwright's career in the context of changes between 1750 and 1900, it seemed as if here there was more emphasis on the concept of causation – why he was successful and which factors were significant in his success. The emphasis on this procedural concept, closely linked to the particular substantive history, was evident in the talk of all our other teachers. Hence both the lessons related to the rise of Hitler were, in different ways, concerned with the reasons for this. For both teachers, what happened in the years leading to 1933 could not be seen simply as a succession of events; they were linked in a web of cause and consequence. Similarly the lesson on the Good Friday Agreement was not just about what had happened in the preceding years but the ways in which these events could be construed as factors leading to the signing of the agreement. Understanding the individual events and movements would enable the pupils to answer the question of why the agreement was possible. The lesson on understanding the possible involvement of the US security services in the assassination of President Kennedy was also about why they might have been involved with motivation as an aspect of causation.

Two of our teachers also spoke explicitly about another procedural concept and its related skills: the use of historical evidence. The lesson on Kennedy was also about understanding the nature of the historical evidence that supported the argument that the security services might have been involved. One of the lessons on Hitler's rise to power, and specifically on the role of propaganda, was also about detailed analysis of forms of propaganda so that the pupils would make sense of its power for German people and thus how this might have contributed to Hitler's rise. In these last two examples, it was especially noticeable how these two teachers' understandings of substantive and procedural history were interlinked. For one, the whole point of the pupils' examination of evidence which related to the conspiracy theory about the secret services in the US was to answer the substantive question, 'Could they have been involved and if so, why?' For the other, looking at the evidence of propaganda was to answer the question about why the German people responded as they did, and hence to consider one of the factors in Hitler's rise to power. This was not sterile 'source work'; there was no hunting out and shooting down of bias, nor meaningless questions about reliability and usefulness. While the sources of evidence used by the teachers and pupils were often interrogated in these terms – What does this show us? Why does it show us that? What doesn't it show us? – this was in the context of a real historical question. 'Doing history' was the focus of these lessons – not 'doing sources'. There would be occasions when some of the distinctive challenges of handling historical evidence would need to be tackled independently – 'those skills, I find you can't rush them and so then you need to break it down in an even more deliberate way' – but not as an activity distinct from understanding how history is constructed.

Two of our teachers made specific reference to the term 'empathy'. Looking at Nazi propaganda was 'beginning to help them [the pupils] to empathise with what the German people were faced with', while considering differing viewpoints about the introduction of the National Health Service was to help pupils in 'empathising about the different opinions of people in the past'. We did not probe what our teachers meant by this term, and previous and current research (Cunningham 2001) suggests that they will have very different understandings of it, but a sense of developing 'the ability to enter into some informed appreciation of the predicaments of people in the past' (HMI 1985: 10) infused much of the teachers' talk. For one teacher, enabling pupils to get into the 'mindset' was important while for another 'you have to realise why it is that people voted for Hitler'. Getting inside the past seemed to be an important dimension of these teachers' understandings of history.

Another dimension of the knowledge about school history revealed by the interviews – and indeed the lessons themselves – was the depth and extent of the teachers' own substantive or content knowledge. Two of our teachers stood out in this respect. The lesson on the Good Friday Agreement reflected extraordinarily detailed knowledge on the part of the teacher, as did the lesson on Kennedy. Interestingly, when asked specifically about this, both tended to either take this for granted or even dismiss it: 'I haven't actually done a lot of reading on it. I think it's something that's built up over time', while in relation to Northern Ireland: 'well I suppose I do but I don't have to make an effort because it's something I'm very interested in'. The implications of this very detailed knowledge base seemed to us most evident in the lessons themselves and especially their questioning: these teachers used that knowledge to ask closely focused questions and to probe pupils' responses.

A final dimension of subject knowledge was that, for several teachers, an overall conception of the discipline was mentioned, even when talking about an individual lesson. For one, 'history is riddled with uncertainties, history is up in the air'. For another,

> the question I ask is am I enabling those children to do good history? That's the most important question that anybody should ask walking in a classroom. And history for me is setting questions, finding out, coming across the problems of methodology, patterns being thrown up that then raise finding out more.

For her, this is contrasted with, 'are you doing enough to enable enough of them to get level 6s'. For both of these teachers this broad understanding was clearly translated into the sorts of subject understandings they wanted to develop in the pupils' lessons. One was trying to understand the nature of the uncertainties associated with Kennedy's assassination, while the other was looking for the patterns in the ways castles changed over time.

Even though we were not asking teachers directly about their subject knowledge, the interviews revealed a great deal. We were particularly struck by the ways in which, for several of the teachers, their understandings of different facets of the discipline – as revealed in these snapshots – were so interwoven. Hence a broad conception of what history is seemed to underpin a more detailed understanding of both the substance and procedures of history, both part of a unified whole. And, as we shall discover when we look at the interrelationships between the different types of knowledge held by the teachers, these conceptions and understandings were intimately linked to what they actually did with their pupils in the classroom – the ways in which their lessons played out in practice.

What sorts of knowledge about their pupils do these teachers seem to hold?

Two sorts of teacher knowledge about their pupils were most evident from the interviews: their knowledge of how pupils, in general, learn and, to a much lesser extent, their knowledge of students' understanding of history. There was also evidence of their knowledge about how to keep pupils on task and engaged, although for several of the teachers this was so closely intertwined with their knowledge of how pupils learn that it was impossible to separate the two. The teachers tended to refer to the pupils as a group, but there was mention of named individuals and even when they were not referred to by name, it was evident that these teachers knew their students well.

Teachers' knowledge about how students learn

For all except one of the teachers, two requirements had to be in place for the pupils to learn. They had to be motivated and they had to be – through whatever means – engaged in the learning task envisioned by the teacher. Motivation was not taken for granted by the teacher and they assumed that part of their task was to find ways of motivating the pupils. For one of the teachers this was one of the key goals of his opening activities in the lesson: 'I'm always trying to think what is motivating the pupils? Just a straight question is not very motivating. It's motivating for those who know the answer, but for the others it's very easy to switch off, and I'm thinking, in what way can you keep people on board?' His answer was a series of quiz-type activities (discussed more thoroughly in the next section of this chapter) which 'gives them a reason for wanting an answer'. These sorts of activities 'get them really hooked and this is all tying up as part of our philosophy'. In a very different way, another teacher used a short extract of video about the Eastern Front and the catastrophes faced by the German forces to 'make the question [of why Hitler invaded] a more interesting one. His greatest mistake, so why? Just a little stimulus like that is actually really nice as a way of getting a little bit of interest into what you're going to do.' Here the history itself was used to motivate the pupils, to encourage them to see the historical question as an interesting one and worthy of further investigation. Other teachers were less explicit about exactly how they went about this process, but comments such as 'I want them to continue to enjoy it because I feel that then motivates them' indicated their belief in this as a crucial ingredient in the processes of learning. Similarly, so too was the pupils' engagement. If the pupils were actively engaged in some way there was a much greater chance they would be learning: 'me talking is not going to give you anywhere near as much', 'that activity will really make them think', 'I want them to do some group work, to share their understanding and to get actively involved. I wanted an active task.' The way this engagement was to be brought about varied for the teachers. For several their own questioning was an important mechanism, but so too were individual, pair or group work tasks: 'all activities they would be involved in'.

Several of the teachers spoke about the importance of learners' confidence in enabling them to learn. For one, this was central: 'they need to feel comfortable', 'they mustn't all collapse at the beginning', 'they have to be made to feel confident, there's no doubt about that'. Without such a feeling of confidence, they would not be able to move on: 'they've become increasingly confident and don't think twice about writing an essay now'. For another teacher it was important at the start of the lesson that the pupils would 'feel comfortable with what they already know', again so that they could move on in this lesson. Another explicitly links confidence to pupils' levels of achievement. When asked about what it was that had enabled the pupils to demonstrate such a sound understanding about the situation in Northern Ireland, she replied, 'well, partly it is developing confidence that they're good at history, which you do right from the beginning'. To achieve this not only are certain sorts of tasks and activities used in the lesson, but the whole curriculum is structured in ways that take account of this. Hence the Year 10 GCSE course begins with the American West which is, for this teacher, 'the easiest topic. They do well and that reinforces their confidence and so they've got a mentality where they can do it and where if they can't do it they can learn how to do it. I think that's the important thing'.

These three ideas about pupils' learning – of the importance of motivation, engagement and confidence – were the three most obviously shared by the teachers. But other themes emerged as well. In three of the schools, the importance of the visual was talked about. Sometimes it was in terms of ways of presenting and understanding information. Hence the form of living graph used by one teacher provided a way of seeing 'more above the line than below the line. I thought the visual impact would be quite useful for some.' For another, the visual representation of pieces of evidence presented as a jigsaw helped the pupils to see that 'the bits of evidence create a whole picture. It creates the idea that these bits together will give you the story you're looking for. But there are always gaps and it helps us ask the question what bits would we like to know more about?' Creating a spider diagram of events associated with Gorbachev's policies created a 'form of visual display that sums it all up'. Such devices were useful not only in the lesson but also as a form of record for the pupils: 'it's a nice diagrammatical way of showing [features of propaganda] that they can stick in their books and refer to later'. For one teacher, the visual, through the use of cartoons about the Nazi–Soviet pact and video images of the Eastern Front, was a direct route into the history. The cartoons showed the ideas about the 'caginess' of the relationship between Hitler and Stalin well, while the video clips offered a direct window into the events of 1941–44.

For two of the teachers, pupils needed the opportunity for 'hands on' involvement if they were to learn. For one, this involved the pupils playing a game in one lesson and, in another, having the opportunity to manipulate information through a form of card sort. For the other, this idea was central to his knowledge about how pupils learn. For him 'that classic Chinese proverb, I hear and I forget, I see and I remember, I do and now I understand' is something that 'I always think about when I am planning lessons. The hands on, it give you an understanding.' So his lessons were replete with pupils doing things, and often working with objects. Included among the forms of evidence about the possible involvement of the security services in Kennedy's assassination were a mock-up of the shirt worn by Kennedy and a model of the Plaza, as 'I wanted to give them something which wasn't just a bit of paper, so they all had something they could use in some way . . . I wanted to give them something to handle'.

The notion that different pupils will learn in different ways was evident in three of our teachers. As one teacher said when asked about why there had been a change of activity in the lesson: 'kids do learn in different ways don't they?' And later in the interview: 'some students – they all learn differently – some need a more concrete approach to some aspects'. One teacher had deliberately planned her lesson in the light of this:

> I want to give them some space. It's their opportunity to verbalise their views in their own way. Some will respond to visual things, some respond to hearing it from other people and some of them respond to independently formulating it through an activity that's actually doing something themselves.

The third, when asked why she had used the living graph, explained 'I'm interested in how different sorts – there are very different sorts of learners' and went on to say why she used the visual image of the graph and how she thought it would be helpful to some. Although their comments here did not make explicit reference to specific pupils, there was a hint of this underlying some of their comments and a suggestion that what they were saying was partly based on their knowledge of how the individual pupils seemed to learn in different ways.

The final dominant idea related to the teachers' knowledge about how pupils learn – intimately connected with their knowledge of students' understanding in history – is their awareness that learning is incremental. Understanding is not a once and for all achievement but a process of coming to understand and thus learning takes place through a series of steps or stages, each of which must be connected to others. Hence, teachers talked repeatedly about the need for appropriate structures which would enable the pupils to build connections. They need 'to move from one level to another quite easily in small blocks' and 'to build connections and bridges in their minds so they can put certain things together'. Such links need to be created within lessons, and as one teacher acknowledged, the pupils had needed more structure if they were to understand the key issues she wanted addressed in her lesson but also across lessons. As one put it, 'we have to have those echo soundings that track through'.

Teachers' knowledge about pupils' understanding in history

While our interviews were rich in data that revealed the teachers' knowledge of how pupils learn in general, it was much more difficult to discover from them what they knew about pupils' understanding of *history*. It may well be that this is a consequence of our research methods: we did not directly ask questions about this. But neither did we ask questions directly about what teachers know about children's learning and yet in talking to us about what they had chosen to do in their lessons and why they were doing it, most talked at some length about this. It may be that their knowledge here is, at least for some of the teachers, so embedded in their practice that they do not articulate it unless specifically probed in relation to it. One teacher said 'I'm always trying to think, from what point of view are they learning? Trying to sit on their side of the desk and think, well, what are they taking from this lesson? What would make it simpler or more obvious for them?' Such a comment suggested a deep commitment to the pupils' understanding in history and constant reflection on what is hard or difficult and what will make it more or less accessible. Similarly, another of the teachers said:

> I know they will understand things on a different level . . . But I've got a benchmark which everybody needs to get. I think in history you can just about play it in those terms. You can have a kind of level understanding that pervades everything and then within that people are able to go further if you can give them the right sort of stuff.

But in neither case did we probe quite what these teachers meant by these statements. What, for example, does it mean to understand things in history on different levels? What makes something simpler? What is the pervading level of understanding in history? Why is that possible? Other current research on history teachers (Cunningham 2002) suggests that at least some history teachers do indeed have very clear ideas here, but to unearth these she had to dig very deep in her questioning and work with teachers over an extended period of time. The picture that emerged for us was a fuzzy one, combining elements of what the teachers knew about school history with what they knew about how pupils learn. Hence what they wanted the pupils to understand was, generally, a reflection of what they knew about the history. Where the teachers had been both very clear and specific about the history embedded in their lessons, so too were they clear about what it was they wanted the pupils to understand. The key in coming to understand these things seemed to be a process of building blocks, with some ideas or skills mastered first and others later. Thus, understanding why Hitler came to power had to be broken down into a number of different reasons and each looked at in turn, so that gradually each factor would be understood in its own right and as a contributory factor in the overall picture. Similarly, to answer the question of why the Good Friday Agreement was possible, a number of different reasons needed to be explored before an understanding of the final answer could emerge. For one teacher, different processes were associated with the stages in building understanding: there was knowledge acquisition, knowledge application and knowledge implementation, while for several of the teachers, developing some sort of base of contextual factual knowledge was clearly a prerequisite for any type of evaluation or judgement. Linking ideas and information was clearly important for the teachers, but quite what the nature of these linkages needed to be was not evident. We are puzzled by our findings here. Many of our conversations with the teachers and our experience in their lessons suggested that they have strong images of pupils' understanding in history and *if* examination results in history are any guide at all to this, the success of former pupils is testimony to the quality of historical understanding developed by these teachers. It may be that our failure to gain good access to this aspect of their expertise is no more than a reflection of our methods. It may be that for experienced history teachers this aspect of their expertise is so interlinked with their knowledge of school history and their knowledge of how pupils learn that it does not make sense to try and disentangle the two. But it may also be that it is an aspect of their knowledge that could usefully be articulated more. Articulating what is hard to understand and why, what is easier, exactly what progress might look like in history in all its forms, what the necessary links are, what the foundation stones are, could all provide the basis for valuable discussion within history departments and especially for beginning teachers. The one clear piece of the fuzzy picture was the notion that students' understanding in history had to be built up and that is something that many beginners struggle with. Often they seem to see student understanding in terms of a once and for all knowledge acquisition event, rather than as a process over time. Our least experienced teacher talked eloquently of her struggle to match what she wanted the pupils to know and understand, how she would structure the lesson to try and achieve that and how she would take the pupils forward. Perhaps more direct knowledge of exactly how experienced teachers construe and resolve those challenges might help her.

Teachers' knowledge about how to keep pupils on task

For most of our teachers this type of knowledge was not, from our interviews, distinct from their knowledge about how pupils learn. Only two teachers talked explicitly about strategies simply designed to ensure on task behaviour by the pupils, but even here there were far fewer references to this than to their knowledge about what would bring about learning. For one, a change of activity could be solely because that would help 'keep the pupils going', or because 'it lightens the lesson', while another activity needed to be very straightforward because 'they're quite excitable'. For the other it was again the knowledge of the need to change activities to keep the pupils on track that was important: 'ten, maybe twenty minutes then change it round'. But what came through most strongly, both from these teachers and from the others, was that it was learning that would get the pupils on task, and hence utilization of their knowledge of how pupils would learn – the importance of motivation, engagement, developing confidence and so on – that would enable them to get the pupils doing what it was that they wanted.

Teachers' knowledge of individual pupils

Although we barely tapped into it, the teachers' knowledge of individual pupils was evidently extensive. In the castles lesson, when the pupils worked in groups throughout the lesson with the teacher visiting each group in turn, the teacher talked about the types of conversation she had had with members of groups and why they were as they were: 'with him, the first thing I have to do is sit him down and calm his feathers . . . I wanted him to have a good lesson but he didn't like being told what he was doing by the girls so I had to get him going'. With others 'they are weak and I need to make sure they're doing something and not just being asked to cut up paper'. And with another, 'I need to get him to realize that he doesn't know all the answers and that he's a little boy with lots of intellectual development to do . . . And that's why I put him with Jamie because Jamie's pretty good and can hold his ground in a debate'. And so it went on – each one of the teacher's conversations had been based on knowledge about the pupils' specific interests, capabilities and what each needed to take them on. Not surprisingly, given the nature of the lesson, this was the conversation that revealed the most. But there were many hints of it in other interviews. Hence, the various forms of evidence used in the Kennedy lesson had been distributed to particular groups as they 'would allow for differentiation, some were harder than others so Mary and Janine got the hardest one', while in another lesson, the teacher was 'thinking, right, certainly him or her would be able to get all those (ideas) and so and so might not be able to do all that but will be able to get this idea'. Occasionally individuals were mentioned by name and a specific contribution they made was mentioned: 'it's very good having him there because you can always get him to start discussions going'. In other cases it seemed that mention of individuals helped the teacher to explain a general principle that was important to them: 'James who's dyslexic and can't write but shows a good understanding orally' served as an example of her knowledge of the different ways in which pupils learn. Similarly for another teacher, her references to individuals highlighted the importance she attaches to confidence: 'Jane, who stayed behind at the end of the lesson, is really quite weak. But she's been asking for additional help and we have been working together – she's gaining confidence and I'm quite encouraged by that.'

Teachers' knowledge about resources and activities

The lessons we saw reflected the availability of diverse forms of resourcing for history lessons and the varied types of activity that are possible. They ranged from a lesson where the resources were many and varied to another in which the resourcing was relatively simple. In some classrooms school-produced resources dominated, in others it was published texts and support materials. Some teachers spoke of using the tried and tested, others about experimenting from year to year. For several of the teachers their talk revealed the strength of match between what they wanted to achieve and the resources and activities they had chosen to use. Several themes emerged from both watching the lessons and talking with the teachers.

The first was the central importance of both the teacher and the pupils as resources in the classroom. All but one of our lessons (and the exception was the castles lesson when the pupils worked in groups throughout the lesson) included a significant amount of question and answer with the whole class, which often developed into discussion. The teachers saw their role here as central, albeit in diverse ways. It might have been to help the pupils to identify key features in propaganda through asking appropriate questions and probing the pupils' responses; it might have been to enable pupils' feeding back to the class to clarify their ideas so that they would become accessible to others in the class; it might have been to check their understanding; and it might have been to reassure their pupils that they were on the right lines. Teachers used themselves to give information, to enable the learners to find out information, to help them make judgements, to enable pupils to share their ideas and to make assessments of their progress. It was not only in whole class question and answer that the teacher was a central resource. Several of the lessons involved the pupils working in pairs and groups and throughout these activities, the teachers were helping both individuals and the group as a whole stay on task and to make progress with whatever the task was. Concomitant with the teacher as a resource were the pupils; their involvement in the lesson was evidently crucial and several of the teachers talked about how their contributions enabled key points to be made and discussion to be moved on.

The second theme is the diversity of resources, and especially activities, in what was a relatively small sample of lessons. All but one of the lessons involved the use of one or more textbooks or associated support materials, although as we shall see these were used very differently by the teachers. All but one of the lessons involved the use of school produced sheets or booklets, and the nature of these varied. Some were essentially to provide information, some to provide particular images or sources of evidence that the teacher wished to use, others offered a mixture of sources of evidence, and tasks and activities for the pupils to complete. Three of the lessons used video: in two watched by the whole class, in another used by particular groups of pupils. One of the lessons involved the use of objects. In terms of activities, question and answer of various types was a central component of the lessons. Pupils were organized in a range of ways – sometimes working as a whole class, sometimes in pairs, sometimes in groups, on occasions on their own. They read, they wrote, they talked, they listened, they watched and they argued. They were asked to extract information, to classify and sort it and to make judgements on the basis of it. Many of the activities involved the pupils having to think and to reach their own conclusions. For example, in the lesson on the Good Friday Agreement, individual pupils were being asked first to find out about events that preceded it, then to make judgements about where these went on an axis of peace to tension and armed conflict and use their subsequent understanding to develop a relatively independent conclusion about why the agreement was possible. In the lesson on the National Heath Service, pairs of pupils had to use the information they had collected about views on its inception to construct a dialogue between a supporter and an opponent. In the lesson on Kennedy, groups of pupils had to assess the extent to which a particular piece of evidence supported or attacked the conspiracy theory of his assassination. In all these lessons, and others, the activities were closely linked together. Hence an initial question and answer might help the pupils to recall what they already knew and take them forward into recognizing that there is now a new issue to investigate. This might then be followed by a reading task to find out information and then a more active task to start using and applying that information, with some form of feedback which shared ideas and enabled the teacher to probe and extend thinking and to check understanding.

In only one school was a published resource the main focus of the lesson. Here it was the John Murray support materials that dominated. In other lessons, published resources were used, but much less and in among school produced materials. Hence, in terms of textbook use, for example, one teacher used two cartoons about the Nazi–Soviet pact (Shephard *et al*. 1993). Interestingly, though, neither of these cartoons were in the section of the book on the Eastern Front – the focus of this lesson – and each was in a different section. The only other uses of the text in this lesson were, first, to ask the pupils to read a page from the section on the Eastern Front after they had finished working on a school produced resource and second, to make a quick reference to a map showing the German invasion plan. In several of the lessons sections of text were used quite specifically as a source of information, with pupils asked to read and extract what was required before going on to use this in another task or activity usually resourced in a different way. In the castles lesson, the text provided an important framework for the lesson in that it offered the questions to be asked about how Chepstow Castle changed over time (Byrom *et al*. 1997) but multiple additional resources were used by the pupils in the group work investigations exploring the answers to these questions. The school produced resources seemed to share a common charac-teristic: they had been designed to match exactly what it was that the teacher wanted the pupils to understand. Hence in two of the schools where it was GCSE coursework that was underway, the school had produced booklets that contained selected information and sources of evidence arranged in their chosen order so that the pupils would be well supported in the independent aspects of their investigations. In another lesson, looking at the features of propaganda, the school produced resource included three examples chosen specifically because they encapsulated the dimensions that the teacher saw as critical to the pupils' understanding.

This matching of resources and activities to goals was evident in much that the teachers said and so too were the ways in which several of them clearly drew on a wide repertoire of resources and activities to make decisions about what would be most appropriate in a particular instance. Hence, even the teacher who said 'I've taught this material so many times now, I know how it's going to go down and what the best way of doing it is' revealed the ways in which he was making adjustments to activities and trying things out: 'in the past I've done that in groups but I thought I would do it as a whole class', 'I don't normally do a question after but I just thought, let's see what they think, because as I was watching it I was reminded of how it does show the features we'd talked about', and 'there's a follow up here that I've done in the past'.

Another of the teachers made frequent references to activities associated with this particular lesson that he had used with other classes in the past and also to the fact that in choosing to use one particular task – presenting pieces of evidence in the form of a jigsaw, for example – he had chosen from a range of possibilities: 'a straight list would have done its job'. It is not surprising that this sense of the broad repertoire of possibilities was most evident in the talk of the most experienced teachers; they have had the time both to develop and use a wide range of strategies and also to see their different effects with a range of different classes and individuals. They have become adept at making choices that will represent a best fit of the potentially competing demands of the needs, abilities and interests of their pupils, the ideas of history, their own interests and preferences, the time of day and what is available.

Two rather different lessons: the moral dimension

Two of the lessons that we saw have not been included in this discussion so far as in each case the teacher specifically identified the goal of the lesson as something other than historical understanding. The Year 9 lesson on the Holocaust was, for the teacher, 'more a citizenship lesson than a history lesson'. For her the value of the lesson was to 'get the pupils to understand what man can do to man and so what their role in the future is in terms of being vigilant'. Although her knowledge of history, her knowledge of her pupils and her knowledge of resources and activities were all apparent in the lesson and in the subsequent conversation, what predominated was her concern 'to set (and maintain) the right atmosphere' and encourage the pupils to 'have a personal response'. What she wanted as an outcome to this lesson was 'a personal response which involved some thinking'. Their response could take any form they liked – prose, poetry, a picture. She was concerned that the pupils should know what happened, how it was allowed to happen and how it was tacitly supported by various groups, but what she was more concerned with was that they should think about 'their own values and what are the values of society'. During the lesson 'I didn't want them to take notes [as they watched sections of a video] . . . I wasn't asking them to remember all the facts, it didn't matter if they didn't remember dates'. What this lesson most revealed is the multiple purposes that might be served by history teaching. Here it was the moral agenda that was important to the teacher and it was in the service of this that she employed all her considerable knowledge and expertise.

In the second lesson, one in a unit on the black peoples of the Americas, the aim for the teacher was 'understanding different forms of racism . . . that racism is not just racial abuse, racial violence, there are lots more subtle ways you can be racist towards other people'. Nearly a third of the lesson was devoted to an initial activity in which the pupils were arranged in a line across a large room, with another line marked on the floor in front of them. They were invited to step across the line each time they were able to suggest an example of prejudice or racism. For the teacher, this physical movement was important: 'I wanted the idea that you're crossing the boundary of what is acceptable by being prejudiced in that way. You're crossing the line.' Subsequent activities involved the pupils looking at contemporary information comparing the positions of black and white peoples in American society so that they could consolidate and extend their understandings of the ways in which racism might affect both groups and individuals. Towards the end of the lesson the teacher introduced the idea that racism might be conscious or unconscious, as he was keen for the pupils 'to look towards structural racism, to get them to think that people don't always think, right, I want to be racist towards this person but there are times when one acts in a racist way because the forces in society are pushing you that way'. What predominated here, then, was the teacher's use of his knowledge and expertise to encourage pupils not just to understand a concept that would be significant in their study of the black peoples unit but also to be aware of 'a real live issue in Britain'.

Conclusion

It is astonishing, at least to us, quite how much knowledge these teachers revealed, especially given the scope and limitations of our research methods. Two key points emerge from this. First, that any attempt to understand teaching cannot rely only on looking at teaching behaviours. Such performance type models of teacher expertise tend to give the impression that teaching is a relatively straightforward job; an essentially technical activity. What our teachers show us is that it is an enterprise infused with highly developed and diverse types of knowledge that are relevant to the task at hand. Second, we believe our simple 'model' of teacher knowledge in terms of three principal components – knowledge of subject, of pupils, of resources and activities – is a helpful way of thinking about this knowledge. Of course, other sorts of knowledge impinge on or are integrated within this: knowledge about the curriculum, for example, and knowledge about the school context. While our model may be crude (and it is), we contend that it can be useful to practitioners and to beginners thinking about developing their knowledge for teaching. It is certainly helpful to us, as teacher educators, in thinking about teacher education programmes.

6 How do history teachers use their knowledge?

Let's suppose that you, the reader, are a history teacher. In the very near future you are going to be teaching a history lesson to Year 7 on the murder of Thomas à Becket. You decide (or you just know because you have made these decisions lots of times before) that you will do it through a form of murder investigation. They will all get a pack of resources and they will open this up in stages. In Stage 1 they will have a drawing of an anonymous body, with some simple labels such as 'long gown made of rough material', 'cross round the neck', 'broken sword on the ground', 'severe wounds to the head and shoulder' and so on. The pupils have to work out what sort of person it was and what might have happened. Stage 2 will involve them looking at a twelfth-century image of the altar at Canterbury and the actual stabbing. The pupils will add to their hypotheses about what has happened. And so on. In making the decisions about what you wanted the lesson to achieve and how you would go about it, you would have been informed by various types of knowledge. Your knowledge about the history will have been significant: you would know what it was about the murder and the relationships between the king and archbishop that you wanted the pupils to understand. Your knowledge of the procedures of history may have been important: you were keen to have the pupils investigate the murder using relevant information. What you know about pupils will have come into play. You know that Year 7 tend to learn successfully through a hands on mystery type of approach and that this particular group are a lively bunch and boredom quickly leads to trouble with them. You know about all the resources that you and your department have created in recent years which you could make use of. In deciding what to do with Year 7 and why, you would have been drawing on all the sorts of knowledge that we identified in the previous chapter.

We saw in Chapter 5 how our teachers' thinking and practice was infused by different types of knowledge. This approach, of looking at discrete types or domains of knowledge, helps us to appreciate the range of knowledge that bears on teaching (Feiman-Nemser and Remillard 1995). But 'at the same time it misrepresents the interactive character of teachers' knowledge and side steps the issue of knowledge use' (p. 14). Using their knowledge about teaching and learning to teach must involve making connections and combining the types of knowledge. As Grossman (2002: 9) suggests, we need to attend to teacher knowledge as a system, rather than as a set of isolated understandings. Various terms for this have been used by other researchers. In looking at the work of mathematics teachers, Ma (1999) uses the phrase 'knowledge packages', while Tobin *et al.* (1990) talk about science 'teachers' mind frames'. In this chapter we want to look at how important decisions about history teaching are informed by different types of teacher knowledge and to do this we focus closely on two aspect of our teachers' practice: their goals for their lessons and the activities they chose to use. We present you with examples of how teachers talked about their goals for lessons and then what they told us about their choice of particular activities. We quote verbatim from our interviews with them. After each set of examples we offer our commentary on what they said and what it suggested to us about the teachers' use of knowledge.

Goals for history lessons

Our interviews with the teachers revealed that they had clear goals for the lessons we observed. They also had goals for each part of the lesson and they offered extensive rationales to explain why they were teaching as they were and what they saw as the purposes of the lesson and its associated activities. Here we focus on their goals for whole lessons.

Two of these lessons – the Year 9 lesson on Hitler and the Year 7 lesson on castles – were typical of the ones we saw. The goals for the lessons were firmly focused on the historical understandings that the teachers wanted the pupils to develop. Most of the goals for whole lessons were of this type. But the two Year 10 lessons reveal other important priorities. In the case of the lesson on Robin Hood the teacher wanted the pupils to understand the nature of film as a source of evidence about both the past and the present. The substantive history – Robin Hood – was important, but so too was a life skill about understanding that films have messages that need decoding. A key goal for the lesson on Northern Ireland was enabling the pupils to cope with the challenges that their coursework would present. Our teachers' goals were not only or just about history: as educators, they had other concerns too.

In each case, it was evident that diverse types of knowledge informed their choices of goals. The teacher of the Hitler lesson was drawing on his knowledge of history and why Hitler came to power, and he was also drawing on his knowledge of the pupils and, specifically, that they might begin with no clear sense of there being *reasons* for this. He was also drawing on his knowledge of the pupils in this particular class and his understanding that for

A Year 9 lesson on Hitler's rise to power

My overall intentions were that they could identify at least one reason why Hitler became popular, something like that. Principally they could see that there were certain reasons why Hitler became popular rather than just, Hitler arrives. That thing about Hitler's ideas, the German economy, and linking with 1920s Germany, and then how, through time Hitler has to do certain things to get to power. So if they can say, well, there's one reason why Hitler came to power, it wasn't just chance that would be my main aim there.

A Year 10 GCSE lesson on crime and punishment involved an examination of excerpts from five Robin Hood films

So it's to look at ideas and to get them to understand that films can have messages. I feel that much of the way teenagers take in information is via films. Reading is not something that they necessarily do a lot, except as a means to an end, in terms of work. So, many of the ways they actually take in information come through the use of film. I'm interested in the use of film historically anyway, so I've got an interest in it myself. For me as a teacher, I'm happier with the book, the written work, but for them, now, Robin Hood will stick . . . they'll always remember that lesson.

A Year 7 lesson on castles

I wanted to do castles because the kids like castles. It's one of those, they like castles, and you have to deliver what the punters like, and that's an issue that comes across in the selection of things that we fit in . . . And I've discovered, I think most of us have noticed it, that the kids who are loyal to you develop in Years 7 and 8. If you look at my AS group, you could almost say, well I knew you were going to take History, you were going to stay with it. And so it was being aware of issues like that. It was also being aware of issues like, I've got to get numbers, because the school finance policy is bums on seats. So there are all sorts of factors like that. Inevitably you pick topics like . . . I want them to address change across time – it is that change across time that I'm doing . . . I needed to give them time to get cracking with the task, and I needed to go round and see how they organised the class because my reason for doing it is chronology, getting kids to map across a period of time, and I don't think we do much in the Medieval period. So it isn't really castles at all. It's chronology and also getting kids to appreciate that things are not going to stay the same across five hundred years.

A Year 10 lesson on Northern Ireland

They're doing their coursework and it's to get them to break down the coursework into manageable chunks, to understand the questions and as a whole we're going to look at one particular bit of it.

In terms of preparing for the coursework, you've designed the coursework, presumably, to what extent do you find yourself teaching to the coursework?

To be honest, quite a lot. And I think that's perfectly acceptable because it's so difficult. They're all going to end up from my experience of previous coursework, they will all end up with something that's different but they do need coaching through it. They need it broken down if you think in terms of literacy strategy, they need it broken down into small bits basically. They need structure sheets, in order to help them work their way through it and it's only when they've worked their way through it then they can look back and hopefully they think 'Oh yes, I do understand how these bits fit together and how I can answer the question.'

Figure 6.1   Goals for history lessons

some, recognizing and understanding just one of these reasons would be enough. The castles lesson was driven by the teacher's understanding of what history is about; for her the key point in doing this topic was that pupils should understand change over time. But it was not only her conception of history that was important. She also drew on her knowledge of the pupils and what they would enjoy. Her knowledge of her context was essential too and she needed to ensure that pupils would be sufficiently interested in history to carry on with it – to become the 'bums on seats' of the future. Her goal for just one lesson was dependent on knowing her history, knowing her learners and knowing her school's priorities. The teachers' knowledge of their learners was most evident in the Robin Hood lesson. The teacher's goal centred around their need to learn how to use film critically and his knowledge of the ways in which the medium was accessible and attractive to them. While there was a sense that his own knowledge and understanding of history, both in terms of the substance associated with the Middle Ages and the use of a particular form of historical evidence are relevant and important to him (and it was evident that he was extremely knowledgeable about the film genre), it was his knowledge of the pupils' lives that took precedence. In the Northern Ireland lesson, knowledge of what the coursework required and knowledge of her pupils united to make a central goal of the lesson a process of breaking down the coursework demands in such a way that the pupils would then be able to navigate a route through. The teacher was aware that the coursework – rather than the history – might predominate, but she accepted this as inevitable if the pupils were to be successful. And as the lesson played itself out, it was clear that both agendas were very much to the fore; while the pupils were being led through the necessary steps to complete their coursework, they were simultaneously making detailed sense of the Good Friday Agreement. Like the coursework, the history too was broken down into manageable chunks. It was unusual to find the teacher's knowledge about the curriculum so evident from an interview about a particular lesson. Our conjecture is that it is partly a consequence of the particular sort of lesson that we saw but also because, while this is clearly an important type of knowledge that teachers hold, it would not often emerge in talking about an individual lesson when the focus was specifically on what had happened in that lesson.

Four teachers, four very different lessons, four different classes of pupils in four different schools. Sometimes the goals for these lessons were driven by the history, sometimes by the pupils, sometimes a particular curriculum requirement. All were affected, in some way, by the pupils themselves. They all reflected the way in which the teacher was juggling a range of concerns and in so doing drew on a range of types of knowledge to make these decisions about their lessons.

Much that has been written about effective teaching either suggests or recommends that having clear goals for learning is beneficial in bringing about learning (see, for example, MacGilchrist *et al.* 1997; Ireson *et al.* 2002). So too does a study that focuses specifically on what teachers and pupils themselves say about effective history teaching (Cooper and McIntyre 1996). Our teachers certainly had clear goals, but to suggest that arriving at these is simple or straightforward is to belie the complexity that is involved. To have clear goals, it seems, teachers need all sorts of knowledge and these need to be combined and appropriate selections made, selections which will, in part, be dependent on particular pupils, at particular points in time, in particular contexts.

Activities in history lessons

In September 2002, a letter written by Corinne Putnam was published in *Teaching History*. She recounts a depressing experience: attending a presentation on the Key Stage 3 Strategy in which a card sorting starter activity, used in geography, was recommended. Putnam describes her reservations about this activity and finishes her letter thus:

> In charitable mood (after all, perhaps I was missing something), I asked how this particular activity was linked to the overarching 'enquiry question'. Where were we going with it? I thought this might shed some light on the geographical thinking it was designed to elicit. To my amazement I was told 'Oh it's not linked to anything. It doesn't have to be. It's just a starter activity to engage the pupils.' Engage them with what?
>
> (Putnam 2002: 7)

In contrast, the activities used by our teachers all had a clear purpose, and the teachers' rationales for their choices were, as with their choice of goals, imbued with diverse types of knowledge. We present just four examples of the activities they used which reveal both the different types of knowledge that the teacher drew on and the ways in which these different types of knowledge were combined.

At first sight, our first example, the quiz, may appear to be like the starter activity endured by Corinne Putnam: just a 'fun' activity to start the lesson. The pupils certainly did enjoy it, but it represented much more than this. The teacher knew that it would entertain the pupils, but his choice was profoundly influenced by his knowledge and beliefs about the pupils, and especially how they learn. Pupils being motivated and having a reason to answer are central and need to be established right at the outset of the lesson. But learning wasn't just about motivation and engagement for this teacher; it was also about the pupils 'digging in their brains'. His knowledge of individual pupils

A quiz

One of the teachers used a quiz type of activity – with the pupils adopting the positions of footballers in two opposing teams – at the start of this lesson on the assassination of Kennedy. The questions asked were essentially recap type questions designed to remind pupils of what groups might have had a reason for wanting to assassinate Kennedy and their possible motives for this.

I'm always trying to think, what is motivating pupils? Just a straight question is not very motivating. It's motivating for those who know the answer, but for others it's very easy to switch off, and I'm thinking, in what way can you keep people on board? So I've got these various sorts of quizzes . . . I've got different aims of class participation in them. With Blockbusters you don't get most of the class involved, you split the class in half, so you tend not to put people on the spot too much, you can ask harder questions in that one. The football one is deliberately designed so that two people have to answer in that certain position, which means the whole group can answer. And it does motivate them, they're absolutely begging, they're salivating at the mouth when they do the football one. Just for basic practice, it's very good for revision, and just saying, well, what do we know? It gives them a reason for wanting to answer, and it also makes you cover a whole span of the class without putting them on the spot. So Grant and John are your strikers, normally they would never answer questions, but they were put on the spot naturally because they wanted to do it, and so it works quite well . . . And obviously you tailor the questions to the person and their ability, easy question, hard question, and it's very good for doing those basic question things again, but I think it keeps them more involved and more attentive . . . I wanted them to dig back in their brains, and that got them to do that.

A practical demonstration

I did a little experiment this time, it's the first time I've used it, trying to recreate the situation in the Plaza, and to really think about these witnesses saying they heard four shots, they heard five shots. I put balloons in different parts of the room. I put one in the back, one over there by the door, one over in the corner. And I got people to put a pin in them after I'd put a pin in the first one. And then I also got a tape recording of three shots being fired, and pressed the tape recorder and did the first balloon, and then the other balloons went off. Then I said, well that's unusual, a bit strange, then just carried on, and I also carried a long brown paper parcel into the room and put it on the desk at the front, which is what Oswald did. On the morning in question he carried a long parcel which he told everyone was curtain rods, and then as we were going through this, I stopped and when we got up to these witnesses here who said they'd heard shots, I said, right, can you tell me how many shots you heard at the beginning of the lesson? And there was a fantastic reaction, only one of them got it right! There were six shots, six noises, but they were saying four or five or seven, they've got no idea, it was fantastic! I said, right, okay, next question, and she said, 'it's from behind him'. Okay, where did the noises come from? Again, only one person got it, they were pointing everywhere. They had no idea at all where these noises were coming from. It was a really powerful example of how you've got to be really cautious. This person said they heard six shots – how do they know?

Figure 6.2 Activities in history lessons

A discussion

If you have mixed ability you have to . . . there are two reasons for discussion. It's a way of testing out students' understanding and in a subject like this it really is very important to test that out step by step because if you lose somebody early on then you've lost them. And number two, I think students learn an awful lot by listening to each other and I think discussion skills are really important and that involves skills in listening at which students these days are not very good.

Using cartoons

It's a really nice way to understand . . . We've done very little work on . . . One of those things you don't make a big fuss of in Year 9 is the ideology of it all, partly because you do a lot more at GCSE level, and it is demanding. Not to get too bogged down in Nazism. So to actually show through the cartoons this idea of two people being pushed together to form a pact, but at the same time being very cagey about their relationship and not particularly trusting one another, and actually I think these cartoons do that quite nicely, don't they? They kind of show up in a straightforward way, when you dissect them a little bit, how they're reacting to one another, and even how this was being perceived by people in Europe at the time. So then through the cartoons we've got the context of, right, we've got this pact, yet at the same time there's the unease that's pervading this relationship, and so we're not going to be too surprised if it all goes wrong.

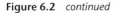

Figure 6.2 *continued*

also emerged. Because of the 'positions' they are given, two boys not only contributed when required to do so but actually wanted to – in contrast to their lack of response to other activities. Although he was not specific about this, his knowledge of individuals also came through in the way in which he was able to tailor questions so that they would be of an appropriate level for different pupils. The teacher spoke at length about this quiz – more than is quoted here – and he made it clear that he has used a range of these types of quizzes, choosing the specific format according to the sorts of class participation he wanted. He knew that particular formats achieve varying effects and he had made a deliberate choice as to which he would use here. He knew too that while these quizzes can prove effective in diverse classroom settings, they are much more successful with smaller classes, and hence with large groups the sorts of principles that inform the construction and use of the quiz are put to a different use (for example, as games – or rather as a complex simulation – about the French Revolution). In his choice of this quiz activity, the teacher's knowledge of history does not seem to come into play. Later in the lesson this was very evident and had a profound impact on, for example, his choice of activities for groups looking at different pieces of evidence associated with the conspiracy theory about Kennedy's assassination. But here different types of knowledge were important and especially his knowledge about the pupils' learning.

The practical demonstration, used by the same teacher, but in a different lesson, again reveals the ways in which his knowledge about pupils' learning informs his choice of activity. For him 'hands on' experience is critically important. He wanted the pupils to really make sense, for themselves, of the potential problems with eye witness accounts and so he turned them into eye witnesses so that they could discover for themselves the important historical idea. But as well as his knowledge of pupils' learning, his knowledge of history was also significant here. Both what he knows about the substantive content – what may or may not have happened in the Plaza that day – and his procedural knowledge of the difficulties of using certain types of evidence about the past were important in him choosing to experiment with this activity.

The first two examples are rather unusual activities, but the choice of discussion as an activity shows us how much knowledge may be embedded in the choice of a relatively straightforward, 'bread and butter' type of activity. The teacher's knowledge about pupils' learning was critical. She knows that learning is incremental and builds step by step. If a step is missed, then the pupil will not make the necessary progress in their understanding and hence her choice of an activity that will enable her to test out their developing understanding. Her knowledge that pupils can learn from each other – and her knowledge of both herself and the pupils as a resource in the lesson – was also evident. There was a hint of her knowledge of the subject too. The Good Friday Agreement is complex and pupils can easily become lost in a morass of detail that makes little sense to them. And finally, there was her knowledge of the pupils' need to develop their listening skills. Thus, a choice that might hardly be recognized as such, of an activity that is commonplace in history classrooms, is attendant on the teacher knowing a very great deal.

The last example shows us especially how the teachers' knowledge of the subject, and the key ideas of the lesson, influenced his choice of a particular resource and associated activity. The teacher chose these cartoons predominantly because they reflected exactly what it was he wanted the pupils to understand – and at the level he wanted it. His own historical knowledge about the key issues associated with the pact came through. We also get a hint of some of his knowledge about how pupils learn in history: that they needed to know where the historical question came from. These cartoons helped to establish that asking a question about why Hitler invaded the Soviet Union is worthwhile. He knew what activity was needed to go with them – a bit of dissection – and it was a *bit* of dissection. As he later says, these cartoons were 'illustrative' and had he wanted the pupils to consider them more as sources of evidence rather than as sources of information he would need to 'break it down much more in an even more deliberate way'. Here he wanted them to understand something about the pact rather than the evidence for it, and hence his choice of resources and exactly how to use it with pupils in Year 9.

The choice of each of these activities is informed by more than one type of teacher knowledge. The teacher draws on and combines knowledge of the pupils, their knowledge of history and their knowledge of the range of tasks and activities that might be used in history lessons. Different types of activity and activities at different moments in lessons seem to reflect different priorities so that certain types of knowledge are privileged at particular points. Activities at an early stage in the lesson appeared to be especially dependent on the teacher's knowledge of how children learn. Two aspects of this knowledge predominated: their understanding of the need to motivate and engage the pupils in what they would recognize as a worthwhile endeavour, and the learners' need for a context in which to situate new historical knowledge. The teachers' knowledge of history, and its influence on their choices, was more evident in the tasks and activities that formed the main substance of the lesson, although it was evident that for different teachers, different types of knowledge were more significant than others. Hence, for one it was his knowledge of how pupils learn that seemed to drive his decisions about activities, while for another, it was his knowledge of history that was central.

In seeking to illuminate the ways in which the teachers used their knowledge, we have focused on their goals for particular lessons and specific activities within the lessons. We have seen how even these individual choices were informed by a deep knowledge base. But with all of the teachers, we were also struck by how each part of each individual lesson, each individual lesson as a whole and lessons both immediately before and after and in the longer term were seen as intimately connected by the teacher. They all strove, in different ways, and with different priorities, to achieve – over time – a variety of different goals associated with children's learning. They were working with a vision of past, present and future. They needed to know where the pupils were in the individual lesson, where they had come from and where they would go next. They deliberately sequenced the curriculum in the light of this, and the significance of this type of knowledge was thrown into sharp relief by our least experienced teacher when she expressed her frustration that 'I've not got the experience, I need to see the whole picture of where they've gone, I can't have an overview yet.' She knew her lack of knowledge limited what she could achieve and her frustration is understandable – it is clearly a very important type of knowledge that she has yet to develop and which must be dependent on accumulated knowledge of pupils, of history, of resources and activities. Sequencing within lessons was critical too and activities and ideas were positioned so that progression in pupils' learning would result.

Bringing about progression is a complicated endeavour. For all our teachers the individual lessons that we saw were, for them, part of a much bigger picture. For most of our teachers, they knew before the lesson started what this picture looked like. A detailed study of an English teacher revealed something very similar and he described it thus: 'backwards building which refers to envisioning where we want the students to end up and then making the plans backwards from there' (McCutcheon and Milner 2002: 91). Similarly, Counsell (2000a) talks of taking a look at 'nice activities', arguing that 'you can get quite a lot out of a random good activity, but how much more can be achieved when pupils' real difficulties are addressed systematically and cumulatively over time' (p. 41). She too concludes with the suggestion for 'backward planning'. Our teachers generally had such a picture of where they wanted their pupils to be and to build towards giving this picture shape and form, they needed to draw on all their knowledge resources. Perhaps more than anything else that we have discussed, this is contingent on the teacher having rich stores of knowledge about their pupils, of the understandings they want them to achieve and of the varied resources and activities that might provide the link between the pupils and the history. The metaphor that stands out for us here is that of building. Diverse materials are employed to construct, brick by brick and step by step, the edifice the teachers want.

Much of what we have discovered about our teachers resonates with what Cooper and McIntyre (1996) discovered in their study of effective teaching and learning, and it certainly reflects what McIntyre has said more recently: 'expert classroom teachers are highly impressive in the complexity of the information that they constructively take into account in order to achieve their purposes' (2002: 127). Cooper and McIntyre emphasize interactions between teachers and pupils. As they say,

> effective teaching [as defined by the teachers and pupils, not the researchers] occurs when the teaching strategy is selected with full regard to the specific circumstances and conditions in which the teaching takes place. Included in the range of circumstances and conditions is a primary regard for students' concerns, perceptions and learning requirements, along with the teachers' knowledge of appropriate learning activities, teaching methods and learning outcomes.
>
> (1996: 131)

We agree. We were also struck by the ways in which and the extent to which our teachers' knowledge of the pupils incorporated exactly the sorts of things that research studies (Cooper and McIntyre 1996; but see too Morgan and Morris 1999; Rudduck and Flutter 2000, for example) on pupils' perspectives have revealed about their preferred ways of learning. Many of the strategies identified by pupils as the ones that they regard as valuable to their learning were exactly what our teachers were employing. Oral explanation combined with discussion and question and answer, use of pictures and other visual stimuli, group and pair work, drama and role play and the use of stimuli which relate to pupil pop culture were all included in the teachers' repertoires. Although we only saw a tiny sample of lessons, it was evident that the use of these sorts of strategies was routine for most. The most experienced of our teachers had deep reservoirs of knowledge about how pupils learn and they were able to draw on those reserves in a systematic way. An additional component of teacher knowledge that we were able to highlight was their knowledge of history. This is not something that emerged from the Cooper and McIntyre (1996) study; that study had different emphases and the time that it was conducted – during the introduction of the National Curriculum – might explain why little attention was paid to this. But, for all except one of our teachers, their understanding of the nature of history and what it was that they wanted the pupils to understand in relation to this was an important and sometimes a central consideration. It profoundly influenced both their goals for lessons and their choice of resources and activities. The picture that emerged for us was one of the teacher mediating history for their learners through the use of specific, deliberately chosen, teaching and learning strategies.

Current initiatives in secondary education, like the Key Stage 3 Strategy, seek to enhance the quality of teaching and learning in classrooms. Literacy across the curriculum, for example, is promoted through ring binders that contain many more or less useful tactics and strategies that teachers can use in the classroom with their pupils. The foundation subjects strand – of particular relevance to history teachers, for the government at least – includes within it an emphasis on formative assessment for learning, with suggestions about how this might be incorporated into classroom practice. But there is scant attention paid in any of these initiatives – however potentially valuable they may be – to the depth of knowledge and belief embedded in teachers' practice. A recent study by Torrance and Pryor (2001) is instructive here. Their intention was to work with primary school teachers (in a collaborative action research project) to see how they could bring about change in classroom assessment, in line with the ideas about formative assessment promoted in particular by Black and Wiliam (1998). It was not enough to offer the teachers the ideas and suggested strategies for them to be able to then employ them in their practice; much more needed to be done. They needed to have the opportunity to work through their existing knowledge and practices to find ways of integrating not just the strategies but all that lay behind them, into their existing understandings of classrooms. As Torrance and Prior say,

> it was not enough simply to make intellectual resources available to teachers; they also have to want to use them. This was achieved through critical study of practice [by the teachers themselves]

> followed by thinking through the use of more flexible and integrated approaches to teaching and assessment.
>
> (2001: 629)

This process of reflection involved the teachers discovering for themselves what they already knew about assessment and its purposes and reconstructing and developing these understandings in ways that would then be consistent with changing their practices. Any innovation that ignores this is likely to founder. So too are innovations that ignore *what* is being taught. As we have shown, our teachers' knowledge of history and their goals for bringing about progression in historical understanding is a critically important element of their expertise.

Many teachers – and certainly all those we worked with – want to continue to be learners. They consistently strive to enhance their teaching. Having the opportunity to reflect on their existing expertise and what underpins this could make an important contribution to their learning. And if there are ideas that others wish them to adopt then we would urge that they take significant account of what teachers already know. After all, constructivist approaches to pupils' learning are commonplace. Why not to teachers?

SECTION 3
Understanding the history curriculum

7 What does school history look like?

You have just been appointed head of the history department in a medium-sized comprehensive school. It is July and you begin your new post in September. Your first job is to look carefully at the history curriculum already in place and decide if, how and why you might wish to change it. But how far are you able to change it? What choices are available to you and to what extent is your freedom of choice constrained by other factors? How do you intend to implement the choices you have made? And how secure are you about the place of your subject within the school anyway?

In this chapter we explore the history curriculum as prescribed by the government and by examination boards, exploring in particular the amount of choice theoretically available to history departments to shape their own curriculum and the internal and external influences which might restrict or facilitate these choices. We then go on to explore how this curriculum is implemented in schools, using the eight case study schools to support the argument that, despite the weight of prescription under which we operate, there is still a remarkable amount of variety and diversity to be found in history departments. Finally, we examine the status of the history departments in our eight schools and set this in the context of wider considerations about the future of the history curriculum. As we return now to the specific details of thinking and practice in our case study schools, we again use the teachers' names.

Choices in the history curriculum

First however, let us return to the new head of department, poised to embark on a detailed curriculum review. She begins at Key Stage 3 and opens up the national curriculum (QCA 2000) to remind herself. She is familiar with its contents, even if she still tends to refer to the British units by their original names (medieval realms, making of the UK, and so forth) and hankers after the days when knowledge, skills and understanding were known simply as the 'key elements'. As with the previous version of the national curriculum implemented in 1995, students must study British history from 1066 to 1900 in a mixture of outline and depth. They must also study a European study before 1914, a world study before 1900 and a world study after 1900. The learning objectives remain broadly the same and the attainment target level descriptions are practically unchanged. So what could this new, enthusiastic head of department do with the Key Stage 3 curriculum if she so wished?

The most recent version of the national curriculum does retain many of its original features. Heads of department have no choice about whether to teach British history or not at Key Stage 3 (nor indeed at any key stage) and the expectation is still that a considerable amount of time will be spent doing so. Furthermore, the remaining three units are hardly free choices given that they must fit into certain broad categories. However, the amount of prescription has been significantly reduced. Each unit has a maximum of three lines of text outlining what should be taught and only one unit (a world study after 1900) refers to very specific events (the two World Wars, the Holocaust and the Cold War). In the remaining units a great deal of content selection is left to the individual department, though it should fit within certain broad parameters. Thus, for Britain 1066–1500, students must be taught 'major features of Britain's medieval past: the development of the monarchy, and significant events and characteristic features of the lives of people living throughout the British Isles, including the local area if appropriate' (DfEE/QCA 1999: 21). On one level, this ensures that certain ground will almost certainly be covered: for example, the Battle of Hastings, the Norman Conquest, and Becket and the Church are likely to feature, with the Peasants' Revolt and Black Death providing some light relief along the way. However, two things make this wording interesting. First, it leaves individual departments and teachers to interpret terms like 'major features' and 'significant events' as they see fit. Clearly, what one Year 7 teacher believes to be a 'significant event' in the medieval period may not be the same view as another's (although years of prescription and numerous textbooks designed to deliver the national curriculum may make us believe that there is an orthodoxy). Second, at no point does it tell you *how long* you should spend on each aspect of the unit and indeed on the unit as a whole. We know from the 'breadth of study' in the current national curriculum that pupils should be taught about 'significant events, people and changes', that they should learn about history 'from a variety of perspectives' and that they should study 'some aspects in overview and others in depth'. But this is as far as the prescription goes.

Clearly then, our new head of department has real choices to make. She can decide what to emphasize within each unit; she can decide in what order they are taught (there is no longer any requirement for them to be taught chronologically) and for how much time; she can choose, in theory at least, any European study and world study before 1900; she can choose whether to teach two units a year or follow a different pattern; she can take a thematic approach to her planning across the whole key stage and start preparing for Key Stage 4 and even post-16. In short, she does have genuine choices to make. These choices might not be comparable with pre-national curriculum days, but the evidence of our eight schools would suggest that even before the 2000 changes, when teachers *felt* that prescription governed them, the choices that teachers made in response to the national curriculum revealed it to be a much more flexible animal than might have been supposed. In her interview, Rachel claimed that, 'I still think there's a lot of choice within them [units at Key Stage 3], I think there always was. And we got very adept at playing around with it, partly because we resented the constraints. I think a lot of people did that too.' Similarly, Tom talked about the national curriculum having 'mapped out' what was a major turning point or incident, but that 'even within that you could make your own choices'. Peter commented that in his planning for Key Stage 3, he was 'directed by the National Curriculum, but there was some flexibility within that' while Sarah admitted that 'sometimes you do need to subvert it for your own purposes'.

The 2000 version of the national curriculum has met with a mixed, though broadly positive, response in our schools. Lucy described it as 'a breath of fresh air really because it's given us all an opportunity to look again . . . I'm glad to see the 2000 curriculum in place. I think it's good news for history and for history teachers and students.'

Reviews of the Key Stage 3 curriculum are evident in several of our schools and while it may be the case that such reviews would have happened anyway, the signs are that in some cases departments are taking advantage of reduced prescription. Some schools have responded more cautiously to the changes, stressing the marginal nature of the changes (described as 'tweaking' by one school). Peter encapsulated both attitudes:

> There's more flexibility in the modules, but you still have to do Medieval Realms, you still have to do Making of the UK, I don't think there's that much flexibility. But we've looked at what changes we might do with Curriculum 2000 . . . The meetings are all devoted to more generic issues . . . Looking at, do we bring out the wider trends between modules? Looking at if we need to extend the breadth of our topic . . . Looking at, do we look at all the perspectives?

At GCSE, much less has changed in terms of choice over the last ten years, with the three syllabuses – schools history project, modern world and social and economic – remaining broadly the same since their introduction in 1986. Those changes which have occurred – for example, a reduced proportion of coursework in 1997, the introduction of a compulsory element of British history in 2000 (which had particular impact on those following a modern world course) and the demise of an unseen documentary paper – while not unimportant, have had less impact on the choices actually available to teachers. Our new head of history therefore needs to decide which syllabus to adopt and which exam board to follow. Then she must choose the modules to teach within the chosen syllabus and set about designing appropriate course-work which meets the exam board's criteria. There is an increasing sense, in some quarters at least, that the GCSE is ripe for updating given the develop-ments that have been taking place at Key Stage 3. Certainly, recent literature seems to suggest that innovation at Key Stage 4 happens despite, rather than because of, the current GCSE structure (Banham with Culpin 2002).

The most dramatic changes in terms of curriculum choice in recent years has been at post-16 level. Here, the impact of the government's reform in 2000 was far reaching and, as always, history proved to be one of the most controversial subjects and was the last to receive official approval from the Qualifications and Curriculum Authority. Prior to 2000, there was an extremely diverse range of choices available in terms of syllabuses, each one offering something distinctive. There were those offering a more traditional route, with two terminal examination papers (for example, one British paper and one European/American paper). Some syllabuses included document work while another included an emphasis on the methodology and philosophy of history. There was a modular syllabus and a syllabus which included coursework, a personal study and a focus on historical inter-pretations. In retrospect, it was remarkably flexible. What has replaced this diversity are three specifications, within which content choices can be made, but in which the overall structure is fixed. In other words, there is less choice in terms of the overall approach and structure than previously. That is not to say, however, that our new head of department has no choices left. She must first decide on the specification to follow and then make further choices about coursework options and, of course, content, ensuring that they fulfil the subject criteria for history published by the DfEE/QCA in 1999. These criteria include a requirement that students should study (for the award of A2) 'a substantial element of British history and/or the history of England, Scotland, Ireland or Wales', 'change over a period of time . . . (at least 100 years)' and 'the history of more than one country or state'. To achieve the AS and the A2, students must, among other things, 'analyse, evaluate, interpret and use historical sources' and 'analyse historical interpretations'.

Our interviews were conducted too soon to gain a proper sense of how the new post-16 specifications were being received (they had not yet finished teaching A2 for the first time) but on the whole, responses were mixed. Sarah expressed some concern about content overload and class sizes which was forcing the department to resort to more didactic styles of teaching once more – 'sorting out post 16 is the mission'. Peter on the other hand, is pleased with the more accessible AS/A2 structure:

> We've made a deliberate change from the A Level. I'm actually quite excited about the new ASs. I had a lot of reservations about the old A Level being too elitist, being too demanding, and it being too unpredictable whether or not the students could do well. Each year, we found some students did well, some students didn't, and I didn't really have a handle on why . . . I'm hoping ASs are going to be different, I'm hoping that once we've a sense of what sort of levels they need to perform at, that we're actually going to be able to get good students to do well and weaker students to do better, that we know whereabouts they're going to hit.

Certainly, the new specifications have caused controversy among practitioners and academics and at the time of writing the whole future of the post-16 (and indeed the 14–19) curriculum is uncertain. Recent developments have encouraged some to look favourably on a British version of the International Baccalaureate.

This summary of the kinds of choices available to heads of department outlined above is not intended to create a false impression. Our new head of department is unlikely to be able to implement all the changes that she would like. Quite apart from the restrictions imposed by the government, a whole set of other factors will intervene to influence and perhaps constrain her choices. This chapter does not explore the more ideological reasoning behind choices as this is more fully dealt with in Chapter 8, but instead moves on to consider some of the more practical, even mundane factors mentioned in our interviews which influence curriculum choices. These factors are divided into those that are largely *external* and those that are largely *internal* although the distinction is a blurred one.

External factors

Resources

Resources were overwhelmingly the most frequently mentioned influence on curriculum choice. Keith, for example, is planning to spend longer on post-1945 in Year 9 on the grounds that 'We've got their new book now which enables one to do that' while Rachel has chosen to teach Northern Ireland at GCSE 'partly because you have to go for the material'. Lucy acknowledged the potential impact that a new series of textbooks could have on the curriculum at Key Stage 3: 'There's no doubt about it, the

Christine Counsell book is very good. It's got a lot of knowledge in it, it has a lot of direction in terms of skills that we want the students to develop and to continue to develop.'

There is also evidence that textbooks can stifle creativity and encourage teachers to teach in the same way year on year: 'since we've had those Schools' History Project books, people get bogged down in six weeks of the causes [of the Civil War]. Why do they need it? They don't. So it's become a notoriously difficult unit to teach for staff.' Similarly, Keith warned that 'if one's not careful, the textbook is so good, that one can use the textbook over and over again, and never do anything different because the textbook works . . . So you've got to be very careful that you're not dominated by the textbook.'

The national curriculum

Another frequently cited external influence on curriculum choices was, unsurprisingly, the national curriculum, although given that it is statutory it was not highlighted as an 'influence' as such – its presence was taken for granted. It would also be fair to say that there was an acceptance of a national curriculum; certainly none of our teachers made a case to abolish it altogether. Interestingly, it was more often regarded in a positive rather than negative light and reference to it was largely in terms of the revised order which provides greater flexibility.

An excess of change

There was a feeling, in at least two of our schools, that too much change was a constraining influence on the curriculum because of the time and energy it takes up. Peter, for example, outlined the various changes his department was in the midst of implementing: new literacy initiatives, changes to the A level and GCSE syllabuses and the forthcoming introduction of citizenship. With so many initiatives at once, he found it more difficult to 'play around' with the existing curriculum: 'the changes that come from outside, I really do feel, sometimes I think, God, how can you expect us to do all this?' Rachel echoed this view and made a plea for less change so that new ideas have time to take hold:

> you will find colleagues occasionally thinking, oh God, I've got to do, say, Cromwell, what am I going to do about Cromwell? What material am I going to use, and where are we going with this? Occasionally, one of us will suddenly think, oh yeah, I remember doing such and such last year. What we need to do is build in a consistency with that, so that kids are having a similar experience across the board and a similar experience across Key Stage 3. But you can't do that when you

have constant change going on, and I'm afraid that's what we have had.

The significance of the local area

Some schools place greater emphasis on local history and trips than others. Where this is the case, the local area has an obvious influence on what is taught. Keith does 'a lot of work on the Church, mainly because of the local nature of having a cathedral, and they've all got medieval parish churches'. Sarah, a strong advocate of local history, teaches Northern Ireland at GCSE partly because of the large Irish population in the surrounding area: 'Historically, the Irish community's been important here . . . one person in the group just went to Dublin to spend time over the half term. They visited the prison . . . so I think it's relevant, it's close, it's often in the news.' The same department has also designed units on the local area which relate to the Civil War, industrialization and medieval towns.

Recent government initiatives, especially literacy and citizenship

All heads of department have to consider how to respond to these current cross-curricular priorities. The teachers we interviewed differed in whether they saw them as an opportunity or a threat. Most appeared to welcome the emphasis on literacy because they could see its potential to improve the quality of history and also because they could see that history's huge contribution to the development of literacy skills could enhance its status within the school. Rachel, for example, referred to literacy as the 'big gun'. There was a more mixed reception for citizenship. More saw it as an opportunity rather than as a threat, partly because of its ability to enhance history's status in the whole curriculum and partly because it provided an opportunity to review and strengthen some of the rationales behind the history curriculum. Keith, however, regarded it as a threat because of a lack of teaching time available for history anyway. Whatever an individual's view might be, however, these initiatives wield a powerful influence on the curriculum, both in terms of what is taught and how it is delivered.

Internal factors

Budgets

The availability of suitable resources has already been discussed, but the ability (or not) to *buy* the resources was also a significant factor in curriculum choices. Keith decided not to teach the Arab–Israeli conflict at GCSE because 'it meant quite a big investment in resources, because we have no up-to-date texts, and

I think now when I look at it, that would have been a very interesting, because young people are so directly involved in it' Keith and Sarah both continue to teach the French Revolution primarily because the textbooks are there and would be costly to replace and Neil decided to continue with the Romans when the national curriculum was revised in 2000 because 'we had quite a lot of resources on it already to be honest'. Departments have had to prioritize ruthlessly; in recent years, the introduction of new post-16 courses forced many departments to concentrate their spending there, perhaps at the expense of the lower school curriculum.

Personal factors

The impact of personal preferences, biases and strengths on curriculum choices was also evident in many interviews. Keith, for example, teaches Islamic civilizations largely because 'one of my own personal favourite topics is the Crusades'. Lucy chose indigenous peoples of North America rather than black peoples of America because 'I spent a year in Canada and my interest which was already quite high has continued since. So it's personal enjoyment.' An awareness of personal bias lay behind Keith's decision not to teach Northern Ireland at GCSE – 'I've got prejudices . . . my wife's a Roman Catholic, so we're a Catholic family, but we have always taken a view that the Protestants are in the majority and six counties are six counties . . . I think in a way I know too much about it.' There was also a desire to play to the department's strengths, especially post-16. Neil has chosen a modern course at A level 'because there are certain people who have certain strengths in the department' even though he would like to see a course where early modern and modern history were combined.

Levels of attainment

Accessibility was important to all our teachers, but it had a particularly significant impact on curriculum choices in two schools. Neil and Lucy both teach the Romans at the start of Year 7, partly because their pupils find it accessible. This is because pupils have already studied it at primary school and it is 'reasonably straightforward'. Neil is also anxious to switch to a different GCSE syllabus because he feels it would be more accessible for the pupils. Keith was anxious both to make history accessible but also challenging. He chose crime and punishment at GCSE, for example, because 'it appeals at the top end to the brightest ones, and at the bottom end, to the less able ones'. Tom had similar reasons for opting – unusually – for Elizabethan England at GCSE:

> It used to be said that the weaker students couldn't cope with it that's why they did American West in other schools and so on. Now we've

not had that problem with that – we've always found that we get good results, even with the less able. But I think there's plenty there to stimulate and challenge the more able. And I felt there's more of that in Elizabethan England than certainly the American West.

Habit

Many of our schools continued to teach certain topics in certain ways because that's what they 'always did'. Keith explained that the structuring of the GCSE course was 'dependent on the way we've always done it'. Tom teaches the Romans in Year 7 mainly because 'well . . . we've done that for some time now'. There were examples of heads of department bringing in topics or syllabuses that they had taught elsewhere. Rachel, for example, introduced China at Key Stage 3 because 'I had done a lot of Chinese history and I was teaching Chinese history before I came here as a Modern World Study, and thought that I could guide my colleagues through that.'

Pressure for numbers

The pressure to recruit well in Year 9 has a definite impact on curriculum choices. Rachel, for example, likes to focus on castles in Year 7 because she knows it appeals to the pupils and may affect take-up of history at age 14. This pressure to recruit also applies at the end of Year 11 and now, at the end of Year 12 too. Peter teaches topics he knows his students will want to study – for example, his students enjoy the elements of American history they study at GCSE so he has included more at AS and A2.

The nature of the school

Apart from the attainment range of a school's intake, there are many other features of a school's population that can influence curriculum choices. Two schools, for example, emphasized their mono-cultural intake in explaining choices such as slavery and Islamic civilizations. Neil, working in an all boys' school, explained how he made the medieval unit motivating – 'we play to our audience. All boys, blood and gore is going to play a reasonably important part, so Medieval Realms is quite a good hook in that.' Mark works in an upper school and the delivery of the Year 9 units is tailored to the needs of the GCSE course. Rachel works in a school which has a very strong English and drama department where pupils follow 'the empathetic social route. That's the route they go down, and so we've latched onto that. So, they want to do local history, and they want social history.'

Models of structuring the curriculum: change and continuity

Once our new head of department has made decisions about what to teach, she then needs to consider how this content should be structured and delivered. At Key Stage 3, for example, she needs to decide in what order to teach the units, whether each unit will be taught separately or whether some will be combined and how long to spend on each one. Table 7.1 summarizes the choices our teachers made at Key Stage 3 and offers a fascinating insight into both the similarities and differences between different departments' approaches.

Overall, the approach in each school, despite the more relaxed attitude of the current national curriculum, is broadly chronological and there were no plans to change this. Foxe School (whose curriculum is organized on an integrated humanities basis) is the main exception to this. Another common feature is the preference in most schools to divide the Key Stage 3 curriculum into six separate units rather than combining any of them together. Although it is not a requirement of the national curriculum to deliver six separate and distinct units, this has, perhaps inevitably, been the approach favoured by most schools. One exception in this sample is Eliot School which in Year 7 places Islamic civilizations after the medieval church and before medieval castles. Otherwise, however, the units remain – at least in the way they are presented in schemes of work – separate and distinct.

That is not to say, however, that these Key Stage 3 curricula lack coherence. A striking feature in many of the interviews were the clear rationales teachers had for choosing certain units or topics and teaching them in a particular order or in a particular way. For example, there was evidence that Key Stage 3 curricula were constructed partly to ensure continuity and coherence across *all* the key stages. In two schools, this was particularly in regard to the development of historical skills. Rachel regarded the introduction of the new AS/A2 specifications as an opportunity to re-evaluate the experience of students studying history up to the age of 18:

> And when the AS came in, I thought, well, it's silly not to use this as an opportunity to actually look at, well, same as the SHP did, what does a kid from 14–16 . . . if they're continuing with their History, in what way should they then be doing it, and what experience should be different?

In two other schools, coherence was also viewed in terms of specific content, where a strong thematic approach to Key Stage 3 linked to the courses offered beyond Year 9. In Foxe School, popular protests – Peasants' Revolt, Civil

Table 7.1 Curriculum choices and structure at Key Stage 3

School	Year 7	Year 8	Year 9
Anderson	N/A	N/A	• Britain 1750–1900. • A world study after 1900.
Brunel	• A European study before 1900 (the Romans). • Britain 1066–1500.	• Britain 1500–1750. • A world study before 1900 (native Americans).	• Britain 1750–1900. • A world study after 1900.
Cromwell	• Britain 1066–1500. • Britain 1500–1750.	• Britain 1750–1900. • A European study before 1900 (French Revolution). • A world study before 1900 (black peoples).	• A world study after 1900.
Darwin	• Britain 1066–1500. • A world study before 1900 (China).	• Britain 1500–1750. • A European study before 1900 (French Revolution).	• Britain 1750–1900. • A world study after 1900.
Eliot	• What is history? • Britain 1066–1500. • A world study before 1900 (Islamic civilizations). • Castles (as part of Britain 1066–1500).	• A European study before 1914 (Romans). • Britain 1500–1750.	• Britain 1750–1900. • A world study after 1900.
Foxe	• A European study before 1914 (Romans). • Children at war. • Britain 1066–1500. • A world study before 1900 (native Americans).	• Britain 1500–1750. • Britain 1750–1900. • Case study on Titanic. • A world study after 1900 (WWI).	• A world study after 1900 (suffragettes and WWII). • What is history? (Mark Pullen)
Godwinson	• Britain 1066–1500. • Britain 1500–1750.	• Britain 1750–1900. • A world study before 1900 (black peoples).	• A European study before 1914 (French Revolution). • A world study after 1900.
Hadrian	• A European study before 1914 (Romans). • A world study before 1914 (native Americans). • Britain 1066–1500.	• Britain 1500–1750. • Britain 1750–1900.	• A world study after 1900.

War, Industrial Revolution, the suffragettes – are emphasized at Key Stage 3 partly because they provide 'a very good link with what they do later on in history', including at AS and A2 where the French Revolution is a major feature.

This thematic approach to the Key Stage 3 curriculum is also evident in Peter's planning. He is currently introducing a thematic study in Year 9 which examines the changing role of women in the twentieth century. It is clear that he thinks in terms of major themes when planning the other compulsory units too. In Britain 1066–1500 'the big thing running through [is] the rise of monarchical authority'; in Britain 1500–1750, 'we make a very big play of the clash between Protestants and Catholics . . . from Henry VIII through to the Gunpowder Plot through to the Civil War'; and in Britain 1750–1900, 'I've been pushing a lot more the issue of the rights of workers'. While these themes, unlike Tom's, are relatively self-contained within single units, it is clear that the 'big ideas' in the Key Stage 3 curriculum have been identified with the potential of real coherence for the pupils. It is also clear that Peter, in common with many of our teachers, regards the Key Stage 3 curriculum as an evolving one. He talks about 'reviewing the curriculum' with his department and 'pushing' certain themes forward.

The other example of curriculum coherence in our schools was the careful placing of units in Key Stage 3. Rachel deliberately teaches Britain 1066–1500 followed by China in Year 7 'as a way of making a comparison between two medieval civilisations. So that's why it's sitting there.' Similarly, Sarah switched from teaching Islamic civilizations to black peoples of the Americas because it fits in with the unit Britain 1750–1900 and in particular, to a visit to Quarry Bank Mill at Styal 'because they see the slave ships and there's a link with the cotton plantations obviously so it almost personalises it'.

So do these examples suggest that the prescription of the national curriculum has stifled creativity or simply channelled it? On a superficial level, the similarities of the Key Stage 3 curricula in Table 7.2 might suggest that the national curriculum removed an intellectual and creative impetus from curriculum planning. The most obvious illustration of this are the optional units that have been chosen. Only two out of an almost endless number of possible topics were chosen for the European study before 1914 (the Romans and French Revolution) while native Americans and black peoples of the Americas dominate the choices for a world study before 1900. Thus, the choices made seem to suggest that even where choice is provided, schools are perhaps reluctant to exploit this, perhaps because of resourcing and also because these are perennially popular topics.

Despite the similarities between these Key Stage 3 curricula, however, it is worth examining the differences. Consider how different Brunel and Cromwell schools are. Both have chosen fairly predictable optional units and both teach the units chronologically. However, think for a moment how the experiences of pupils in each school might differ. The curriculum in Brunel

School is perhaps the most typical of all schools, both in terms of choice and structure. Pupils begin with a study of an ancient civilization, the Romans, whom they have encountered before at Key Stage 2. British history plays a significant role in all three years of Key Stage 3 and forms the bulk of study in Years 7 and 8. The non-European study – native Americans – introduces pupils to a wholly different culture and tackles the tricky issue of colonization. By contrast, in Cromwell School, pupils essentially end their study of British history early on in Year 8 and concentrate on European and non-European units at a point when they are becoming more intellectually and emotionally mature. Another feature of Cromwell School's curriculum is a much greater emphasis on recent history than in Brunel School, not least because the whole of Year 9 is dedicated to the twentieth century. The key point here is not that one model is somehow 'better' than the other, but that within the confines of a national curriculum there can be so much variety. In the absence of empirical evidence, it would be unwise to claim that pupils from Brunel and Cromwell schools might end their Key Stage 3 history studies with clear differences in terms of their knowledge and understanding of history (and perhaps to some extent the world in which they live) but that nevertheless remains a possibility. Add to this the differences in pedagogical approaches, treatment of historical concepts and skills and resources and the obvious differences in the experiences of pupils who all, in theory, receive the same curriculum becomes clear.

This supports the distinction that has already been made between the 'standardised and theoretical curriculum' and the 'local and actual curriculum: the curriculum which is daily negotiated teacher to child and comes alive in the classroom' (Bage 2000: 44; see also Ball 1992). No matter how prescribed the curriculum, central government's control over education will always be diluted by other influences, including LEAs, schools, departments and individual teachers who appear, even if they did not realize it at the time, to exercise what Phillips (1998) aptly describes as 'creative conformity'. With less prescription at Key Stage 3 than ever before, departments are now freer to experiment with the structure of their curriculum. And although our teachers were taking a piecemeal approach to reviewing Key Stage 3 (having been recently preoccupied with make major changes at post-16 and, to a lesser extent, at GCSE), publications aimed at practitioners have clearly indicated the kinds of creativity that can be applied to planning both across and within units (Counsell 1997; Riley 2000).

In order to establish a clear structure for the delivery of the history curriculum, history departments produce increasingly detailed schemes of work which outline what should be taught and when. In pre-national curriculum days, these were often presented in the form of a list of topics to teach in a given term. Schemes of work are now far more sophisticated and include, for example, careful cross-referencing to national curriculum objectives and cross-curricular opportunities. Table 7.2 provides an extract of exactly this kind of scheme from one of our schools. The content is clearly divided into themes or 'key issues' and questions. There are also three overarching foci identified at the beginning. The concepts (which include both procedural second order concepts such as 'change' and substantive concepts such as 'Catholic') and skills (which include both specifically historical skills such as evaluation of evidence and more generic ones such as decision making) are there because they are inherent in teaching the content. They are a means to an end and not an end in themselves. This reflects and supports the arguments made in Chapter 6 that the most experienced and effective practitioners do not make a distinction between the content and the skills because they are inextricably interwoven with each other.

The idea of structuring a unit of work around a series of 'big questions' which drive sequences of lessons was popularized in textbooks published after the national curriculum was introduced and especially in the Schools History Project series (for example, Shephard *et al.* 1993) which remain popular and well used in departments across the country. Many of the 'big questions' are now enshrined in history schemes of work throughout the country, such as 'Was Guy Fawkes set up?', 'Should Dresden have been bombed?' and 'What did Elizabeth really look like?' The notion of structuring sequences of lessons around a single question is now most popularly known as 'enquiry-based teaching' and has gained widespread popularity through articles in *Teaching History*, (for example, Gorman 1998; Riley 2000). Several of our schools have adopted the approach. The central feature of enquiry-based teaching is that pupils are encouraged to engage with substantial historical questions which require critical thinking, problem solving and reference to primary evidence to answer. Enquiry-based teaching and learning is perhaps becoming the 'new orthodoxy'; it certainly poses a challenge to the potentially fragmented approach encouraged by the 'double-page spread' mentality of early national curriculum textbooks and what has been termed 'death by sources A to F' (Counsell 2000a).

The position of history within the broader curriculum

One of the questions we asked our teachers was about the position of history within their individual schools. Did they feel that history had sufficient status? Out of our sample of eight schools, they divided roughly in half in terms of an overall positive or negative response, although overall the answers were more optimistic than this might indicate. Not surprisingly, those schools that enjoyed the highest uptake at GCSE and AS/A2 and the best examination results were the most positive and confident about their position in the school, although it was not possible to determine which came first, the optimism and

Table 7.2 Extract from Key Stage 3 scheme of work, Godwinson School

Lesson No.	Key issues	Content and approach	Key elements (See Table 1.2)	Concepts	Skills	Links with other subjects
1 and 2	Establish continuity with medieval Britain and a base against which to judge changes	*English society in 16th and 17th centuries. England in 1500s* Class discussion of what England was like under these headings: population, towns, jobs, houses and furniture, food, social groups. Written work to follow. Could be in chart form, comparing these features 1500/1994.	1, 2, 5	Continuity and change	Analysis of evidence Comparison	Geography
3 and 4	Importance of religion in lives of ordinary people and in national politics	*Religious change in 16th century – when was the English Reformation introduced?* 1 Introduction to Tudor family (use time line) 2 Emphasis on importance of religion in both ordinary people's lives and national politics. 3 Discussion of what 'Catholic' and 'Protestant' mean. *Was Henry VIII Catholic or Protestant?* • Class discussion of evidence p. 28 and divide it under 2 headings – Catholic and Protestant • How did his problems lead to this confusing action? Do you think he was Catholic or Protestant when he died?	1, 2, 4, 5	Catholic Protestant Monastery Dissolution Reformation	Evaluation of evidence	R.E.
5		*Why did Henry close the monasteries?* NB Refer back to work on Stoneleigh Manor re. monastery. Discussion of evidence pp. 29–30. Does the evidence show monasteries closed for money, because they were corrupt or for other reasons? Students work in small groups and report back decisions.	1, 2, 4, 5	Monk Monastic vows Motivation Causation Reformation	Decision making	R.E.

confidence or the good results. Certainly, the quality of teaching appears to have a profound effect on the strength of the subject and concern was expressed in three of the schools that non-specialist teaching was detrimental to the subject's image. After good teaching, high numbers beyond Year 9 and good results, the next factor most frequently linked to high status was the attitude of the senior management. In two schools in particular, this was seen as crucial:

> We are very well protected here because the head values the Arts subjects and the Humanities. There are no compulsory languages, there is no compulsory technology. If those two things were the case, we would be sunk without a doubt, or we would certainly struggle to maintain anything like we are at the moment, and I know in schools where they have done compulsory language, compulsory technology, then you have history, geography, business studies, sports studies all competing for one slot, and it's so difficult. Whereas here we are, despite other subjects coming on line, and quite rightly, we are in a fairly protected position, and that will continue.
>
> (Mark)

Similarly Rachel felt that history's strong position is partly due to the support of the headteacher, himself a historian:

> we have a head who is a historian, and I think among our school governing body there's an emphasis on academic work and a willing-ness to support it . . . We wouldn't go down the Technology College or the Language College road, or the Arts College . . . so that's not going to be a threat to history.

However, active support from the senior management was not regarded as a vital factor in the high status of the subject in Cromwell School where the emphasis is more firmly centred on the quality of teaching and results. Of course, the relationship with senior management is often affected quite considerably by the results tables. As Rachel put it, 'It [the status of history in the school] depends on the relationship the Head of Department has with the management, and whether the department is delivering the goods or not. I think we are delivering the goods . . . in terms of results.'

Interestingly, Rachel felt her optimism partly to be based on the fact that her school was unlikely to go down the specialist status route, while Neil's sense of vulnerability was in part due to the fact that his school already had. Working in a technology college had left his department feeling marginalized, both in terms of the way it is perceived and in terms of the physical environ-ment, with poor teaching rooms.

Another factor identified as a threat to history's status was a perception by the students that history was somehow 'harder' than other subjects, which had a knock-on effect on recruitment at GCSE in particular. In fact, in half our schools, more pupils choose geography at Key Stage 4 than history, partly, at least, because of this perception. This is particularly the case in lower-achieving schools where levels of literacy are relatively low, but it is also the case in higher attaining schools. There was general agreement among our teachers that history is (and has to be) a demanding and challenging subject, but they all shared a firm commitment to making it accessible to all. Sarah summed this up well:

> I think the very nature of history is very difficult. That isn't to say that kids can't do it. And it's partly the value of history, isn't it, if you think of those skills, transferable skills, the humanity core, evaluating evidence, understanding very difficult history concepts, you know, what you're doing is giving them all of life skills. It is hard.

The overall impression was that in general, history does not attract the lower attainment range as much as some other subjects, although that is not to say that it does not attract pupils from across the range. Keith acknowledged that 'we get better girls. And we do better [than Geography] at the top end' while Sarah, although sure that history GCSE groups represent the full range of abilities, realizes that more vocational subjects such as business studies attract a higher proportion of lower attaining pupils.

The amount of time allotted to history in the whole curriculum was raised in several of the interviews but was not discussed as frequently as we might have predicted. There is certainly considerable variation in the amount of time given to history at Key Stage 3 (see Table 7.3) though slightly less so at Key

Table 7.3 Curriculum time for history at Key Stage 3

School	Hours per week history teaching at Key Stage 3	Per centage of curriculum time at Key Stage 3 devoted to history
Anderson	1 hour 30 mins	6
Brunel	1 hour 30 mins	6
Cromwell	1 hour	4
Darwin	1 hour 45 mins	7
Eliot	1 hour 45 mins	7
Foxe	2 hours	8
Godwinson	1 hour 40 mins	6.5
Hadrian	2 hours 20 mins	9

Stage 4. Lucy's department has more than double the time at Key Stage 3 than Peter's, though interestingly, this does not relate to the status of their departments in the wider school curriculum in the way one might expect. In fact, the amount of time each history department has, while having obvious ramifications for the kinds of approaches each adopts, does not, surprisingly, appear to reflect the status in which it is held in the school. So, for example, Peter, who has the least amount of time at Key Stage 3, is very confident and positive about the position of history within the school.

In terms of our individual schools, therefore, the status of history in the wider curriculum and the confidence felt by our teachers varied. When asked about the future of history in schools more generally, it was a very different story. Only one of our teachers felt mainly positive about this; the remaining seven expressed several concerns. Perhaps most surprisingly of all, some of the schools in which history is thriving were among the most worried about history's future. Mark, for example, whose department is one of the most successful and popular in the school, had this to say about the future of history in the school curriculum:

> I think it's pretty bleak, to be honest. I think there's something about way the subject is often presented, and the way it's often organised – in schools, outside of schools – which has got a kind of dusty feel to it still. I don't think the subject has necessarily moved on in the way that some other subjects have. I think with developments in vocational education in schools, as well as a range of other appropriate courses coming on line, it's having to compete, and I don't necessarily think it's competing particularly well, or it's being able to. I think it will survive, but I just don't feel that the position is particularly secure.

Similarly, Rachel and Sarah, both working in highly successful departments, were concerned about the potential threat that specialist status might pose to history departments. Rachel, while positive about the place of history in her school, was much less positive about the place of history in schools generally. At the end of the day, she said, 'from talking to other colleagues I know who are in technology schools, where the money is not there for history at all – schools I've had to lend books to before now . . . I think it's down to the local features of the school you're in'. Sarah would agree, and is worried about the implications for history if her school were to become a technology college. Meanwhile, Peter's main concern is 'that I'm not convinced there are enough quality people coming through to take the baton forward'. Other concerns were raised about the possible marginalization of history within the curriculum and an 'overemphasis' on the core subjects.

Overall then, views on the future of the history curriculum in schools were fairly bleak. There were positive comments scattered in among the negative ones – for example the opportunities afforded by citizenship to increase the status of the subject, the more flexible curriculum at Key Stage 3, vastly improved resources – but these were in the minority.

Conclusion

Our new head of department has many curriculum choices to make, even though these choices must fit within the demands of the national curriculum and examination syllabuses. The choices made in our schools demonstrate how different the experience of a pupil studying history in one school is from a pupil in another. There are, of course, a number of factors – both internal and external – which will influence the choices our new head of department makes, although we did not sense that the teachers we interviewed felt unduly constrained by these. What our new head of department could learn from the experience and expertise of our teachers is the extremely thoughtful rationales that lie behind their curriculum planning. There was a tremendous sense of coherence in these curricula on a number of levels; our teachers chose units, emphasized certain topics and themes within these units and placed them carefully within the whole curriculum for good reasons. Perhaps in part because of this, our teachers spoke warmly and enthusiastically about their curricula, an enthusiasm which echoed their positive reflection about individual lessons. Such a positive outlook was absent from their reflections on the future of the history curriculum and not all feel secure about the place of history within the whole school. There is much, therefore, that our new head of department can feel positive and encouraged by, but she needs also to be mindful of the need to defend the status of her subject and to rid it of any traces of 'dustiness'.

8   What is school history for?

Chapter 1 has already explored how the developments in history teaching since the late 1960s reflect shifts in how the *purposes* of the history curriculum have been articulated. The 'great tradition' of history teaching – which prevailed for most of the twentieth century – regarded history as a means of transmitting important messages about national identity based on notions of a shared cultural heritage and a progressive development of democracy. History was a body of knowledge to be imbibed by pupils encouraged to be passive, unquestioning learners. It was a body of knowledge that was largely made up of British (and, more likely, English) history with occasional forays into Europe and the Empire. The 'alternative' or 'new' tradition which emerged in the late 1960s and early 1970s radically challenged these assumptions about the purposes of history in three ways. First, learners were regarded less as passive recipients of knowledge and more as active participants in the learning process. Second, the content of the history curriculum was questioned by those who embraced 'new' and 'hidden' histories and who wanted the curriculum to reflect broad social changes leading to a more multicultural, plural society. And third, the procedural knowledge of history – leading to what John Slater eloquently described as 'the crucial distinction between knowing the past and thinking historically' (Slater 1989) – was promoted as a key contribution to pupils' wider development, both in the whole school curriculum and beyond. History, then, was gaining an extrinsic justification; it could help pupils to make better sense of the world around them and to become active, tolerant, critical and informed citizens.

The teachers in our sample are obviously products – and champions – of the 'alternative tradition'. Indeed, not only have they been greatly influenced by the approach pioneered by the Schools' Council History Project in the early 1970s but they also largely accept the national curriculum for history. They may be critical of it at times and wish there was less prescription, but they do not argue for a return to the days with no prescription at all. This does not necessarily imply, however, that they advance identical justifications for the history curriculum in schools. This chapter offers an analysis of how our teachers defined the purposes of the history curriculum. Its intention is not to offer any judgements or to speculate on the direction the history curriculum might or should follow in the future. Rather, it is hoped that, as Martin Booth wrote in his similar study of history departments over 30 years ago, 'the practice of other history teachers can be of value in clarifying our own thinking' (Booth 1969: 9).

The chapter is organized into five sections, each of which analyses the interview data according to the following themes:

- Does content matter?
- Moral education and political literacy
- The procedural knowledge of history
- Enjoyment and accessibility
- History and outcomes

During the course of the analysis – which for this chapter, focused on the second interviews about the whole curriculum – it became clear that several common themes were emerging in what the teachers were saying. Prior to conducting the interviews, we had no clear sense of the themes which might appear, nor indeed whether there would be significant similarities between different teachers in different schools. Perhaps fortunately, striking similarities did appear and while different teachers placed different emphases on these various themes, we are as confident as researchers can ever be that the themes do reflect the kinds of issues that were raised most commonly by our teachers.

Does content matter?

It is not the purpose of this section to revisit the familiar debate of content versus skills which – alongside the related debates about British history – dominated media coverage of the history curriculum in the early 1990s. Chapter 1 has already provided an overview, and a thorough account of this 'great history debate' can be found elsewhere (Phillips 1998). The old arguments do, of course, resurface from time to time, but the crude distinction between historical knowledge and historical skills – which teachers themselves rarely, if ever, made – is now thankfully less frequently drawn. The teachers we interviewed did not concern themselves with a 'skills-against-content' approach and there was generally an underlying assumption that the two are inextricably linked. Despite a commitment to a skills-based approach, content *does* matter a great deal to our teachers. This was demonstrated by the detailed and thoughtful theoretical rationales offered to explain the choice of some areas of content over others. What is interesting, however, is what our teachers had to say about the *selection* of content. The content or knowledge of history, they argued, should provide the opportunities for particular sorts of learning, but they were uncomfortable about claiming that *particular* content should be taught. This should not, however, be confused with an argument that content therefore 'doesn't matter'.

A prescribed curriculum?

There was a marked reluctance among our teachers to answer the question 'Are there topics which you feel must be taught at Key Stage 3?' On the whole, our teachers were extremely cautious in advancing any firm views about what content should be taught *in general*. They could argue why they felt *they* should teach particular content, but they were uneasy about broadening this out to apply to everyone. Their choices were down to 'personal judgement' and 'one person's choice is not the same as another's'. Some regarded prescription with suspicion, equating it with political control: 'My philosophy, my view on that has always been, as much as anything, to allow as much choice as you can, because I think the minute you start prescribing topics, this is when history becomes the political football idea in a way.'

Our teachers did not feel that the purpose of teaching history was to provide essential knowledge of particular times and places and they were more comfortable with the notion of selecting content on other grounds, for example the development of critical skills and particular values. Sarah claimed not to be 'a strong content person' and was unable to argue for any particular prescribed content unless it helped to 'deliver this cross curricular dimension like, say, studying the Holocaust because I do think history needs to be a vehicle for students to bettering their values and their understanding of the modern world'. Peter argued that the main point of studying history 'is not about remembering the key facts, it's about understanding things, it's about analysing, it's about being able to do things, as well as providing a general skill in life'.

Despite these arguments, however, most of our teachers reluctantly went on to identify certain areas of historical knowledge that they felt children 'ought' to know about because of their intrinsic historical importance. These choices were largely based on two criteria: the concept of the significance of an event or a period – implying some kind of long-term impact and a fairly clear link with today's world – and the idea of possessing a broad 'sweep' of knowledge which could provide pupils with a historical framework. One of the periods most frequently identified as 'significant' was the Middle Ages and, in particular, 1066. Variously described as 'essential', 'a very important period' and a topic which 'should be there', several schools argued for its place in the history curriculum because of its long-term significance: 'it [1066] is the changing point in our history, our nation. The Normans brought certain things which, if they hadn't come, would have made us a very different kind of country.' Other 'significant' events included the Reformation, the Civil War, an aspect of 1750–1900 (there was less unanimity on this, although slavery, political reform and social change were among the topics mentioned) and the two World Wars. One school argued the case for the Romans – 'a key development period' – and another for Elizabeth I – 'a crucial point' – but other than that, no further topics were deemed significant enough to make their place in the curriculum self-evident. It is important to stress, however, that the schools were responding to a hypothetical question about what *they* thought should appear in the history curriculum, a speculative question we have all considered either publicly or privately. They reflected and were able to respond articulately and coherently. But they did so with an equal measure of humility and, the argument above still holds true, that as a group they were clearly reluctant to be too specific about content and were unanimously in favour of less rather than more prescription. As one teacher put it, 'There are certain things that I feel have a good call to be there, but I wouldn't fight to the end to say they've got to be there.'

In terms of a general 'sweep' of history, the arguments were more about a pedagogical approach – teaching through overviews as well as depth – than about defining what content pupils should be taught. Mark felt that 'the key point is that they should be able to emerge from school at 16 or indeed at 14, if they choose not to study beyond that, with at least a real flavour of the way the history of the world with people has developed'. For him, pupils ought to have 'some sort of flow of time' and they should end the compulsory study of history with knowledge of 'what actually happened, how it panned through'. Rachel echoed this view:

> I don't think you're a historian if you don't have that sweep, if you don't have some familiarity with the Roman period or the Medieval period or the Tudor period or whatever you want to call it. I think those are important. I think there's a chronological pattern that needs to be there.

That did not mean, however, that they were advocating specific content. Rachel went on to argue that 'I don't see particular subjects I think children should be taught' and Mark summed up the problems inherent in our question by asking

> Are there things the kids should know about? Well, yes, but where do you start and where do you stop? Should they know about the Holocaust? Yes, they should, but then, should they know about slavery? It's where you begin and where you want to end it.

Not all teachers were comfortable with the notion of a 'sweep'. One in particular argued that 'maybe this is a sign of a failing teacher, but I don't think pupils see the big picture. I don't think a Year 9 student can see the development of England and say, these are the main things.' Earlier in the interview he made it clear what he did think was possible:

> Ultimately it doesn't really matter to me what knowledge they come out with. There are a few key things that yes, they should know, but ultimately they have to come out being able to handle it, being able to analyse, being a thinking person, that's ultimately what I'm trying to create. I think History does that more than anything. Well, a thinking and a literate person. So ultimately, forget the facts, I've forgotten what I did at A Level history and I'm a specialist historian now.

Interestingly, a similar debate emerged in Martin Booth's study. Then, as now, history was taught chronologically and Key Stage 3 contained broad sweeps of British/English history. But one of Booth's teachers felt that, 'in practice, whatever one does children are too young to be expected to have a great deal of time sense' and another argued that, 'the making of a time chart doesn't particularly appeal to me and of itself is not particularly valuable unless you want to hammer some point home into its historical perspective' (Booth 1969: 15).

Clearly then, there are areas of disagreement among our teachers about what is and is not possible in terms of content but ultimately, what binds them is their reluctance to be dogmatic about what should and should not be taught. For them, the selection of content is both highly personal and also subject to goals other than knowledge of history itself (more of this later). Variety was another important influence on their choice of content and they were highly sensitive to the charges of an over-emphasis on the twentieth century and were anxious to make their curricula broad and varied. Lucy felt that in her experience, 'students end up doing twentieth century in Year 9, twentieth century at GCSE, twentieth century history at A Level and they go on to do it at university, and I wanted a breadth and a depth of what I see history to be'. This was a view shared by at least half the schools interviewed and was a factor in their choice of the Schools' History Project syllabus at GCSE rather than the modern world option (7 out of 8 of our case studies schools follow this syllabus, a figure which does not correlate with the national trend).

History and identity

The place of British history in the national curriculum was fiercely debated in the late 1980s and early 1990s (see Chapter 1 and Phillips 1998) and the debate still goes on, albeit in a more muted form. Those people – largely termed the 'new right' – who consistently argue for greater emphasis on British history in the curriculum usually do so on the grounds of national identity, pride and common cultural values. Often their arguments have been advanced alongside an exhortation to teach children about national heroes and heroines in order to instil a sense of pride and confidence in their country's achievements (Tate 1995). In the event, the national curriculum for history in all its incarnations has largely escaped the kind of uncritical and narrow 'version' of history that this could potentially have involved. Nevertheless, British history has remained a strong presence in the curriculum at Key Stage 3 since 1991 (and in fact became an even stronger presence in 1995 when a non-British compulsory unit was dropped) and has now also secured a presence at Key Stage 4 and post-16.

What do our teachers make of this? When pushed by us to identify those things which 'should be taught', they identified only British events, which would suggest a belief at some level that pupils 'ought' to know about key moments in British history. This was rather at odds with what they had to say explicitly on the subject of British history. They were unanimous in not wanting more, and almost unanimous in wanting less. Most would choose to include more world history in their curriculum if possible and, while acknowledging the significance of certain events in British history as outlined above, were generally quite suspicious and wary of it. Peter spoke of an 'Anglocentric' national curriculum, Neil – a Scot – spoke of the 'horrific focus on English history' while Rachel argued that there was 'no such thing as English history' anyway! Sarah expressed it most strongly, combining a rejection of both the broad sweep approach and also an over-emphasis (as she saw it) on British history: 'I'd be happy to ditch some of the British history . . . I don't think you need to romp through British history from 1066 to whatever.' While none of our teachers advocated dropping British history completely, there was a strong sense in all the interviews that a bit less would free up the curriculum and enable more European and especially world history to have a stronger presence in the curriculum. The stronger presence of British history at Key Stage 4 and post-16 did not go unnoticed. Mark regarded the compulsory study of British history post-16 with dismay, pointing out that

> these kids are beyond school age, they can leave school if they want, no-one's saying they've got to study anymore, and yet they're being told compulsorily, that they must do some British history! Now that to me . . . is an invasion of their liberties, isn't it?

Thus, the concept of history as a means of cultivating identity, national sentiment and a common cultural heritage – so central in the 'great tradition' of history teaching explored in previous chapters – was almost entirely absent in our interviews. Interestingly, Neil associated prescription partly with political attempts to foster national identity and regarded it with considerable suspicion:

> I'm very torn between the idea of exploring things that are just fascinating, but then you're always bringing your own biases in, your own preferences. The idea of how much we should be giving the students some sort of sense of national identity, whatever that means, and at the moment I have no idea to what extent we should be instilling some kind of understanding of ... the more it's pushed on by the government, the more I think it's a bad thing.

> *It's interesting that you associate that phrase with content, national identity.*

> Certainly in the first National Curriculum, there were specific people that were mentioned, so I think content is immediately linked to national identity. Things like, Nelson and Wellington, all that sort of stuff.

The ambivalence of our teachers towards British history – at once identifying British events as most 'significant' while also regarding them with suspicion – is a trait which is itself perhaps very British. In countries divided by internal conflict or only recently formed, the notion of an established, relatively uncontested national history would doubtless be embraced and promoted, not regarded with some suspicion and wariness. This is not intended to imply that a greater emphasis on our 'national past' would be a good thing; rather it is an observation about the complicated relationship we have with notions of 'Britishness' and, indeed, 'Englishness' and the ways this relationship manifests itself in our views of what history should be taught in schools.

Moral education and political literacy

Throughout our interviews, there was an abundance of comments about the 'relevance' of history to the modern world. It was a term used both to justify history's place on the school curriculum by enhancing a child's understanding of the world they inhabit and to explain how history can be made to engage and excite pupils. No one claimed that history does – or should – attempt to shape future generations. But there is no doubt that our interviewees regard history as potentially transformative, that is to say, that it can play a modest part in creating tolerant, empathetic, responsible and questioning citizens. The appearance of citizenship as a statutory national curriculum subject seems to have encouraged many schools to re-evaluate the contribution history makes to what we might term moral education and to political literacy. Many departments have had the chance to claim parts of the citizenship curriculum as the right and proper domain of history; some have embraced this opportunity, others have resisted or viewed it with more suspicion.

History and moral education

The extent to which history teachers should view moral education as a legitimate aim has been subject to debate and not inconsiderable disagreement. At the heart of this debate lies a crucial distinction between those who believe that history brings with it its own intrinsic goals (for example, Lee 1991) and those who challenge the notion that 'knowledge for its own sake' is possible – or desirable – given that knowledge has to be selected and therefore certain criteria must be applied (for example, White 1994). Lee accepts that history is transformative, but he argues that it is the pupils who change, not society as a whole. Therefore, the argument goes, history should not be made hostage to goals extrinsic to the discipline itself. 'Good citizens' and 'socialization' are 'contested slogans, not appeals to historical criteria' (Lee 1991).

There is no doubt where most of our teachers stand in relation to this debate. The majority of our teachers used the language of moral education to articulate their views on the purposes of the history curriculum. The kinds of values informing their curriculum choices and their teaching in general were transparent, drawing on notions of plurality, diversity, respect for humanity and fundamental tolerance combined with an understanding of how individual action can impact on others either negatively or positively in profound ways. To borrow from a discourse that has informed so much of citizenship education, the perspectives we encountered in the interviews therefore combined ideas of rights and responsibilities, in other words, the rights to freedom and the responsibility of others to help defend and protect that freedom. To this extent, then, our teachers assumed a set of shared values. Perhaps none of this is very surprising. After all, what is history teaching about if not to make judgements and how is this ever possible without a degree of moral reasoning? (Arthur *et al.* 2001) As Slater writes, 'Judgements and moral attitudes lie at the heart of historical language' (Slater 1989). How, for example, can we teach the slave trade or the Holocaust in a moral vacuum? (Husbands 1996). Should we be presenting the case *for* Auschwitz? (Slater 1989). Choices have to be made about what to teach and how to teach it and, for most of our teachers, the kinds of moral reasoning and social values it can thereby promote were an important factor in these choices. What was less clear was the extent to which the teaching of values such as toleration, respect for diversity, understanding of different attitudes and beliefs should be approached entirely historically or linked more explicitly with issues specifically relevant to today.

Difference

One very important criterion applied by our schools in their curriculum choices was that of 'difference', that is, the importance of studying a society whose ideas, attitudes and beliefs differ significantly from our own. Lucy talked about the unit on the Romans as 'an opportunity . . . to try to get a sense of studying different peoples of the world, particularly people outside of their own experience of Britain', while Rachel chose China 'because it was completely different'. This links, of course, with the enthusiasm for non-British history already noted previously. It also links with a commitment to develop skills of empathy among pupils. Our teachers were committed to exploring how other societies differ as a way of promoting greater understanding of difference more generally and therefore a greater acceptance of the diversity of societies today. Lucy teaches the indigenous peoples of North America because 'a lot of pupils perhaps aren't exposed to exactly what a native American is . . . It's very interesting this work in challenging their own perceptions, looking at stereotypes, prejudices', while Keith teaches Islam to Year 8 because:

> we face an enormous amount of prejudice within schools. Increasingly the Muslim world is very important to us. Again, if you're going to understand the world you live in, you really do need to know something about Islam. From a national point of view there are increasingly going to be Muslim politicians, Muslim leaders in government. They are going to be increasingly significant in the world that we live in.

This argument is based on an (unproven) theory that understanding about different societies in the past might reduce fear of such difference and in turn, encourage greater toleration and respect for diversity today. It would be extremely valuable to have empirical research available which explores this theory further. Two of the schools were acutely aware that their own populations were mono-cultural and that the need to explore other cultures was consequently more pressing: 'we're very aware that we're not a multi-ethnic school. We're very aware we've got a duty, both a moral one and an educational one, to try to broaden their horizons.'

A different approach, but one which is ultimately intended to produce the same learning outcomes, is to use history, as Lucy put it, 'as a warning'. The most common topics at Key Stage 3 which exemplify this approach are slavery and the Holocaust. Peter teaches black peoples of America in order that pupils:

> Think about racism and discrimination . . . That's certainly our purpose – to broaden their horizons, get them aware of racism and make sure that they're aware of the dangers and pitfalls of it.

So is that almost history as vehicle?

Yes, it is. That's quite explicitly why we chose it in the first place. We had clear discussions about it, we took a long time to plan that module and I'm very pleased with it. Sort of, what are the dangers here and what do we have to try to avoid, and that's what's behind that one.

Similarly, Keith teaches slavery because 'It's very important for them to know why black people live in this country and have a right to be in this country in a place like x, where people see this like some alien culture being implanted. It's not like that at all.' And Mark explains 'You look at slavery, and there's a whole moral dimension to that, and basic issues about how human beings treat one another and so on.'

Teaching history 'as a warning' is not straightforward, however. It is not simply a case of teaching children about what is right and wrong. Both the histories of slavery and the Holocaust can raise uncomfortable issues about complicity and human fallibility. Keith explained how pupils find the study of anti-Semitism in Germany 'uncomfortable'. It frightens them because they are forced to confront difficult questions about human behaviour: 'They assume it's just all about Germans, the German people, then they begin to understand the pressures, and they start saying, what would I have done? How would I have reacted in this situation?' The very fact that genocides have happened more recently, a point often made by teachers when teaching the Holocaust, is evidence enough that acts of evil carry with them some dark and troubling messages about humanity. Pupils prefer to believe that things get better over time and history can challenge this. Keith encounters this very issue when he teaches crime and punishment at GCSE:

> They don't like it sometimes, because they want a study in develop-ment to be about progress, things getting better, and this isn't. This isn't at all. Sometimes it seems a lot worse over periods of time, and it challenges this assumption nearly all of them have got, that life gets better.

History teaching, then, makes things more rather than less complicated and this is one of its greatest strengths. It raises issues of causation, con-sequence, motivation and interpretation. It challenges children's view of progress and humanity. It provides a context in which to explore some of the fundamental issues facing society. But how far should history teachers assume the role of moral instructor? There was a general sense in the inter-views that history teachers are not in the business of preaching. At the same time, however, a slight difference of opinion arose about how overtly values such as toleration should be taught. Mark believes that:

> When we deal with that [slavery] – when I deal with that, and I get the feeling how we work on it as a department – we don't start with the presumption, or with the statement, rather, that this is wrong and we're going to look at how awful it is. We start with a little bit of the context of the time, this is what happened, there are your conclusions, draw them yourself. Absolutely the same when we tackle the Holocaust in Y11. It's like anything. I think we've got to allow our groups the opportunity to realise these things and come to these conclusions from an historical point of view, rather than, wasn't this so awful? Well, of course it was, but you know, the danger of starting from that position rather than an historical position.

Essentially then, Mark believes that the appropriate route for a history teacher is to present these topics neutrally as they would any historical topic, providing pupils with the evidence on which to base their judgements. He is certainly not alone in his view (for example, see Kinloch 1998). Sarah, by contrast, rejects this approach entirely, arguing that history is 'not about teaching kids facts, it's about getting kids to make judgements on facts, how could you make a judgement on the Holocaust outside a moral framework? No.'

On the whole, the approach of most of those teachers who discussed this issue lies somewhere between these two positions, though with a slight bias towards Sarah's. We have already seen, for example, how Peter approaches the black peoples course as an anti-racism one and Keith teaches Islam specifically to challenge existing prejudice. Similarly, Neil teaches the Third Reich from a 'history as a warning' perspective, exploring issues such as 'Why were people attracted to Hitler? How could they fall under his spell?' All of them combine history and – for want of a better term – moral education. The importance of the historical context is vital, as are the usual concepts and skills you would normally deploy – interrogation of the evidence, reasoned and substantiated argument, empathy and so on – but the intended learning outcomes, based partly on issues about morality today, are transparent and made clear to the pupils. According to Davies (in Arthur *et al.* 2001) this is not necessarily typical among history teachers. He argues that most teachers regard what we might term 'citizenship issues' as less important than the development of knowledge about the past and the development of skills for understanding the past. The specific example he gives is human rights. However, a majority of the teachers we interviewed did not justify topics which were essentially about human rights in terms of the historical understanding they developed. Even Mark, who consistently emphasized the importance of a historical approach and the development of historical skills in the interviews, was clearly aware of other possible outcomes when teaching topics such as slavery and the Holocaust:

as far as the way we look at our scheme of work, each area has a skills area which it's focusing on. Within that, and quite interestingly, one of the areas which I am quite interested in looking at in terms of the way we look at our scheme of work, is aspects of other cross-curricular areas which will of course in the by-product of study in the past come into it. We don't really ever do that, I feel, particularly explicitly.

Political literacy

So far in this section we have explored the extent to which our teachers regard the fostering of certain values to be an important purpose of the history curriculum. This in turn reflects their concern that history should be made 'relevant' and help to prepare pupils for the adult world. A different way of looking at this is, of course, in more political terms. Do we have a responsibility to be engaged in political activity at a local or national level and to understand something of the world around us in order to make reasoned and informed judgements? There are many ways in which an individual might contribute to public life. The Crick Report used the term 'political literacy' in its broadest sense – as 'preparation for participation in public life' (Arthur *et al.* 2001) – and, as we have already outlined in Chapter 1, it is clear that the Advisory Group for Citizenship envisaged that history should play a substantial role in this respect. Five of our schools had explicit things to say about history's role in developing political literacy, although there was some disagreement about how overt the relationship between the two should be.

Most of our teachers claimed that history helps pupils to understand the present in some way or another. However, five of our teachers laid particular emphasis on understanding the world politically. This involved providing pupils with the right kinds of knowledge and understanding, as well as the essential 'life skills'. Tom, for example, chooses areas of the curriculum partly on the basis that 'there are things there that they can learn that I perceive to be important about society today, political ideas about society in general' and teaches communist China because:

> I wanted to do an area of the world that they didn't know much about, that was important, that was increasingly going to be important, to make them . . . informed citizens of the future. I always say this is a reason why you should do history, you're going to be voting soon and you need to know about world-wide issues and potential conflict situations and things like that.

Similarly, Rachel argued that the only absolutely essential component of the history curriculum was the twentieth century because:

> We thought we should do, the nature of democracy, against dictator-
> ship in its various forms. The role of media. Media in History. You
> know, all these flipping American films they make which are howling
> mistakes or whatever you want to call them. So I would say there are
> aspects of the 20th century you should study. I wouldn't particularly
> say you should study the Atomic Bomb. I think rather you should
> being studying the current nuclear power club, or whatever. And the
> Holocaust, I don't know. I think that's an aspect of state power, and
> how it can be used.

The role of the media, nuclear power, state power – these are as much
terms to describe our current preoccupations as our old ones. This is history
designed to engage pupils in debates which have a direct and political
relevance with today. And it isn't only twentieth-century history that can
accomplish this. Keith's approach to teaching Robin Hood, already described
in Chapter 6, was partly to draw some parallels between government policy
then and now. Sarah takes an even bigger responsibility to promote active
citizenship through history:

> I've got a mission I suppose to get kids to see politics not as party
> politics but . . . that they should feel empowered, that they're not an
> individual on their own, that it matters, they have a say and that you
> should never . . . never assume you haven't or never assume that what
> you say won't have an effect.

This is one of her aims when teaching Northern Ireland at GCSE; she hopes it
will 'get kids to extrapolate from that and to think more widely and hopefully
to get an interest in the world they live in'.

Not all our case study schools were comfortable with the notion of
political education, however, or at least not in an explicit form. For some, the
political understanding and values which can certainly emerge from a study
of history should remain relatively implicit. That does not mean to say they
are not deemed important, or that they are not a conscious factor behind
curriculum choice and delivery. Lucy demonstrated this particular relationship when she was discussing Year 9 lessons on democracy and dictatorship.
On the one hand she hoped they would 'draw the logical conclusions and they
would therefore maybe feel more confident, more able to participate in the
political process than maybe they currently do' while on the other she felt
that 'I don't see it as the role of the history teacher, I do think it is very
important going back to this idea of context.' Similarly, Imogen, when asked
about political education, wanted to stress that for her, history is history – 'I'm
very cautious about then trivialising it into a sort of citizenship' – but that
nevertheless, political understanding can be a valuable by-product of history.

The contrast between Sarah and Karen's positions in terms of an overt relationship between history and citizenship, already identified in Chapter 1 as one of the professional challenges currently facing teachers, is one that will doubtless continue to spark debate as citizenship becomes more firmly entrenched in schools.

The procedural knowledge of history

So far we have mainly focused on the rationales behind content selection. It is plainly obvious that no two people will ever agree on what content should be taught. We all have different notions of what the criteria for the selection of content ought to be. Some us approve of broad sweeps; others favour more studies in depth. Some want to preserve British history, others want much less of it; some want to teach those things which lend themselves to debates about morality and those things which make a 'good citizen', others prefer to justify their selection with aims more intrinsically 'historical'. Content, then, can never be objective and value-free. Fortunately, the procedures of history can (Slater 1989).

The teachers in our interviews frequently used terms like 'skills' and – less often – 'historical concepts' when discussing the purposes of the history curriculum. They assumed a shared understanding of these terms and rarely defined what they meant unless specifically asked to do so. Their definitions – while perfectly sound in terms of their individual objectives – demonstrated that these terms can be somewhat slippery and unclear. The distinction between concepts and skills were on occasions blurred while 'skills' as a term encompassed both what we might regard as 'core historical skills' such as working with primary evidence, constructing a balanced argument, making judgements and writing analytically, and skills which we might more broadly define as 'life skills' such as critical thinking, independent thinking, working productively with others, ICT and literacy. The distinction between 'core historical skills' and 'life skills' is hardly a clear one with many examples of skills which are both 'core historical skills' and 'life skills' – clear communication might be one, for example. Nevertheless, it is worth noting that there is a slight, although discernible, difference between those teachers who regard history as invaluable in developing 'life skills' and those whose priority is to refine core historical skills in order that pupils get better at doing history. This latter camp would not dispute the relevance of historical skills to the wider world, but the wider world may not, in the first instance, be their main concern. It is a subtle difference, but one worthy of note.

Conceptual understanding

The procedural concepts most frequently mentioned were causation, change and empathy. The latter is particularly interesting because of its non-existence in official documentation and the criticism it generated in the 1970s and 1980s. While it may, as a term, have fallen out of favour in official and academic circles, it has clearly remained an important element in the teaching of history. Euphemisms have been sought and found; the current national curriculum orders for history refer to pupils being taught 'the relationships between the characteristic features of the periods and societies studied including the experiences and range of ideas, beliefs and attitudes of men, women and children in the past' (DfEE/QCA 1999: 20) which must surely require a significant amount of empathy to achieve properly. Indeed, it is difficult to imagine history without empathy. The use of imagination to recreate the thoughts and feelings of those in the past are central to understanding the past (Husbands 1996) and this is a position that most of our teachers would thoroughly endorse. They used the term empathy liberally and unapologetically; what was less clear is quite what they meant by empathy – current research would suggest that definitions vary (Cunningham 2002) – and this was not something we chose to probe further, though it would doubtless have been interesting to do so.

What is also worthy of note is the consistency of our teachers in terms of the kinds of conceptual understanding they emphasized. Other than causation (and consequence), change (and continuity) and empathy, interpretations and similarity/difference were also frequently mentioned. All these procedural concepts owe a great deal to the work of the Schools History Project and indeed, two of our teachers acknowledged its influence on their understanding of history teaching. This may tell us as much about the age of our interviewees as anything, but also reflects perhaps how much the national curriculum owed to the groundwork of the SHP.

Life skills

Five of our teachers used the term 'life skills' when discussing the purposes of history in schools. These included questioning the world around them, thinking independently and critically, evaluating all the evidence before reaching a judgement and striving for balance. One teacher's aim is to foster 'questioning citizens', another wants to develop 'enquiring minds'. Tom hopes that through history, pupils 'gain . . . the skills of looking at things in a balanced way, evaluating evidence before making judgements. As I always say to them; "this is propaganda", these are important life skills and no other subject but history teaches them to that extent.'

What underpins all of these comments is a desire to educate young people to be interrogative, critical and independent in their judgements; to investigate and gather evidence; and to reach their conclusions only on the basis of this evidence which is carefully weighed up and evaluated. Lucy expressed this at its most extreme: 'students need to be aware of exactly that nothing is essentially, necessarily true'.

Core historical skills

If five of our schools emphasized the importance of 'life skills', the three remaining teachers could be described as promoting 'core historical skills' in particular. This is, in fact, too crude a distinction; all eight teachers would argue that they developed both. But it became apparent when analysing the data that three teachers – all of whom teach in high achieving schools – emphasize the skills necessary to getting better at history more than the others. For example, Rachel felt that:

> At the end of the day the baseline is, am I enabling those children to do good history? And I think that is, to be honest, the most important question that anybody should ask walking in a classroom . . . and history to me is, setting questions, finding out, coming across the problems of methodology . . . and patterns being thrown up that then raise more finding out.

Similarly Mark had this to say:

> The things that we're concentrating on particularly – again, this is where they cut across each other in KS3 and GCSE – ability to explain why things happen, the causation side of it. That again is a crucial element, the 'why' questions which dominate both still, if they go on to GCSE and indeed A-level. To recognise changes and continuities. To appreciate evidence in the way historical evidence works, and the way it can vary and be used in a variety of different ways. To empathise with people in the past. To organise their ideas in an historical way, to be able to present information in a way which is understandable to the rest of the group, and so on. Those sorts of things.

Interestingly, both teachers, while placing the greatest emphasis on 'core historical skills' because it's 'what historians do', were also among the most critical of 'sourcework' which they regarded as a necessary, but rather dull, part of history. Mark feels that 'preparation work on evidence' is not 'the most enjoyable thing . . . it's quite demanding and not always the history they really want to do'. Similarly, Rachel admits to 'fighting shy' of sourcework: 'The kids hate it, which is probably a reflection of how we feel about it.' The view that evidence-based work is not the best way to inspire children was echoed elsewhere, but overall the messages were contradictory. Peter is 'trying to fight against the idea, which a lot of students have, that we're doing sources, so it's not quite as interesting'. And Rachel, quoted above, later talked about the 'buzz' generated by enquiry work when pupils are given a freer rein to conduct their own enquiry using evidence. Perhaps this approach, currently championed in recent school textbooks and editions of *Teaching History*, isn't yet fully equated with 'sourcework', possibly because one can be fun and the other is rarely so. The heavy emphasis on public examinations in Anderson School and to some extent in Darwin School, both of which have extremely large numbers taking GCSE and which have a reputation of high results to maintain, could perhaps be one explanation why 'sourcework' is approached with some reluctance. It is perhaps also a sign of how GCSE is now lagging behind Key Stage 3 where good teaching is now characterized by enquiry-based learning where evidence is integral to answering substantive questions. This is a far cry from the 'compare and contrast' and 'how reliable/useful' types of questions which still characterize GCSE examination papers. If this is the case, then until the enquiry approach is adopted not just in GCSE teaching but in the public examinations, the use of evidence at Key Stage 4 will continue to be viewed as 'sourcework', with all the negative connotations we encountered in our interviews.

Enjoyment and accessibility

Enjoyment

All our teachers regard enjoyment as an important purpose of history teaching, though for slightly different reasons. For Lucy, teaching in a school which draws on the most deprived catchment area of all of our schools, enjoyment was all about confidence building, whereas for Mark, teaching in a school with high take-up at GCSE and outstanding exam results, enjoyment was also about recruiting Year 9 pupils to GCSE. Of course, all schools would agree that confidence building is important and that good recruitment in Year 9 is vital. But the difference between Lucy and Mark was quite striking and reminds us about the impact of different contexts on teachers' views. Somewhere in the middle was Peter who, when reflecting on a record 80 students in taking history in Year 12, said:

> People are feeling comfortable with the subject, they're feeling that they can cope with it, and they're obviously enjoying it, that seems to be coming across pretty strongly. So that's been a really positive sign. That's one of my overall aims, just to make history enjoyable, just to

> get kids in the classroom and saying, this is bringing it to life, this is something which I can relate to and understand and really enjoy.

So how does the idea of enjoyment and pleasure affect choices about what is taught and how? Three of our teachers explained curriculum choices specifically in terms of pupil enjoyment, though no doubt it is a factor in all schools to some extent. Rachel teaches Germany 1919–45 as the depth study at GCSE rather than the American West – which she actually prefers – because 'the kids actually like Nazi Germany'. Similarly, Peter has chosen modules on civil rights and war in Asia and the Korean and Vietnam wars in Years 12 and 13 in order to build on the very popular work done lower down the school: 'So students . . . will see Civil Rights, USA extend itself in the Vietnam War in Year 13, and they'll say that's for me. And it's worked incredibly'. For Lucy, pupil enjoyment is a deciding factor at every level:

> I think what I've done more in the last year, 18 months, is to follow the students more. To perhaps lessen my preference and go with what the students enjoy and allow them to do good history, and allow them time to pursue their interest. It seems to be more worthwhile at the end of the day.

Clearly then, choices about what to teach are based partly on what pupils will enjoy.

Accessibility and inclusion

Our teachers demonstrated a tremendous commitment towards making history accessible. Literacy was the subject of much discussion, particularly in four of our schools: 'you can't be a good history teacher without being aware of literacy'. The two schools with the lowest GCSE scores – Brunel and Hadrian – were, not surprisingly, the most concerned to raise levels of literacy among their students. Neil is now 'having to put a heavier emphasis on literacy' while Lucy says that 'It's [literacy] a huge factor [in planning], it should be anyway, but it is a huge factor here.' For Rachel, literacy is the best ammunition history has for maintaining its status in schools and increasing departmental allocations. At the same time, however, literacy is also 'part of the commitment that history has . . . the kids are not trained history writers, it would be ridiculous to expect them to be'. Notice here how improving literacy means high level writing skills. Although many of our teachers advocate the use of discussion in class it seems as though this is a means to an end, rather than an end in itself. In other words, discussions may help pupils to understand the topic better rather than also developing and refining oral skills. A similar case could be made of reading. This would suggest that our teachers emphasize writing as an outcome of history above – and perhaps to the exclusion of – anything else.

Encouraging participation was an important aim of the history teacher according to our teachers. Lucy wants students to feel that history is something 'that they can participate in' and Sarah agrees, frequently stressing how much she believes pupils learn and gain confidence from each other. Peter is keen to hear that 'students do feel comfortable answering questions and saying things' and he is aware of how issues about gender – specifically the absence of women from the history curriculum and the underachievement of boys in the school – might mitigate against this. He intends to introduce a thematic study of women in the twentieth century and has made specific curriculum choices in an attempt to engage boys and encourage them to achieve more: 'The thinking that, the more boys were engaged by a topic, the more they would try to do well at it'.

There was unanimous support for the continuation of non-tiered papers at GCSE although concern was expressed about the literacy levels on some of the examination papers. Peter, for example, argued that:

> The language levels and the depth of knowledge they're expected to get, are just absolutely appalling . . . the readability level of one of the questions is 15.11 . . . I just think it's absolutely outrageous they've a question in that's 15.11 and loads and loads of my Year 11s are nowhere near, and we're making a really big push to try to make it accessible to all students.

Similarly, Mark complained about the 'wordiness' of the exam papers. While he accepts 'historical terminology' such as 'interpretations and reliability', he objects to phrases which might disadvantage certain pupils:

> but terms like 'changed out of all recognition'. Now for some of the weaker ones, 'changed a lot', or 'changed greatly', fine. The use of terms like 'dramatically' and 'generally' and 'demonstrate' and things like which aren't necessarily the language of the historian, but which are built into questions, which actually have a massive impact on what they can write.

History and outcomes

A 'pre-occupation with outcome-led management' has already been noted in Chapter 1. Heads of department are under increasing pressure to provide a raft of assessment data for internal and external scrutiny. The pressure to move level 5s up to 6s and grade Ds up to Cs is increasing in some schools and national interest in league tables ensures that the spotlight on external examination results is intense. To what extent, then, was this pressure reflected in our interviews?

Of course, the importance of good examination results, especially at GCSE, was seen to be of undeniable importance in all our schools and certainly one of the purposes of the history curriculum in schools. The reasons, however, were two-fold. On the one hand, results were regarded as crucial by some to the status of the subject in schools; without good results, heads of history could lose their influence with senior management and the subject could become less attractive to parents and students. Keith, for example, declared good results to be 'very important' because without them, the headteacher would limit the number of GCSE groups to two. On the other hand, however, good examination results were also regarded as a pupil's entitlement. To fail to secure good results was to fail the pupil:

> obviously the end results are pretty key, they're up there. If I was to put things in order of priority, I'd say, students are coming to us to do the subject in order to get a GCSE which is going to take them somewhere else. And so, results have to be the number one thing, and I'm really pleased with how the results are going.

Similarly, Mark talked of results as important 'because otherwise we're doing them a little bit of a disservice if we're not properly preparing them'. At the end of the day, achieving good results is in everybody's interest, from the pupils to the senior management and beyond. Certainly, there were signs that the delivery of the history curriculum is profoundly influenced by the demands of external examinations. In one school at least, the curriculum at Key Stage 3 is seen primarily as a preparation for GCSE. In another, the style of teaching changes noticeably at Key Stage 4 and becomes much more content-driven:

> I wouldn't say I'm teaching history at all. I'm teaching to the exam. I don't think there's very much room for enquiry or debate. It's very much, these are the packs, you need to regurgitate them in an exam.

The pressure to cover the content at AS Level was mentioned by two of our teachers – 'We're having to look more to making sure they've got the content' – and Sarah in particular felt that the amount of content which needed to be covered in Year 12 was forcing the department to revert to more didactic styles of teaching and argued that pupils were now 'over-assessed'. We can see, therefore, that the drive for good results is seen to be a fundamental responsibility of history teachers. In turn, this has a profound effect on the way the history curriculum is delivered. None of this is really very surprising, but it would be misleading to omit any reference to external outcomes in a consideration of the purposes of the history curriculum. At Key Stages 4 and post-16 at least, part of the point of studying history is to obtain a qualification.

On a final note, it is worth mentioning how few teachers talked about national curriculum assessment as a particular influence on the way they delivered the curriculum; enabling pupils to achieve high levels was not, it would seem, regarded as a purpose of history, or at least not one that deserved much attention. Only two teachers referred to national curriculum assessment/attainment levels in the interviews and both were rather dismissive about the attainment levels as ends in themselves. Rachel argued strongly that what mattered at Key Stage 3 was whether pupils were 'doing good history . . . Not, are you doing enough work to enable x number of level 6s . . . I don't think that counts at all'. Similarly, Sarah does not want assessment at Key Stage 3 to be 'a stick that you're beating them [the pupil] with . . . I would not want a system where 'you've got to do this because you've got to get up to a level'. Most schools assess pupils against national curriculum levels throughout Key Stage 3 – despite advice from the QCA that the levels are only really of value at the end of Year 9 for a summative judgement – and increasingly this is to meet the request for data and targets by senior management. But in our schools at least, the achievement of high national curriculum levels did not figure largely in their discussion of their aims for Key Stage 3 history. Perhaps in contrast to the anxieties in the early 1990s, assessment at Key Stage 3 is now regarded as a useful diagnostic tool rather than as an end in itself which dictates what is taught and how.

Conclusion

All our teachers held clear views on the purposes of the history curriculum and there was considerable similarity between them. The choices made about the curriculum were clearly informed by these ideas. Extrinsic justifications for the history curriculum were often articulated and our teachers were comfortable with the notion of history partly as moral and political education. There may have been disagreement about how overt and explicit this relationship ought to be, and certainly some of them also advanced more intrinsic justifications for the subject, but, nevertheless, they felt this wider purpose of history teaching to be valuable. They were similar, also, in their reluctance to be dogmatic about content and in their preference for less rather than more British history in the curriculum (though certain contradictions did arise in this respect). In discussions about both the *content* they teach and the procedural knowledge that informs the *way* they teach, our teachers demonstrated a firm commitment to the importance of both. There were no 'distracting dichotomies' (Counsell 2000b) here. Finally, our teachers wanted their pupils to enjoy their history; they wanted pupils to participate in their lessons; and they wanted history as a subject to be inclusive. Examination results were seen as important not just to please senior management and meet government targets, but also as an entitlement for pupils. At the centre of our teachers' views about the purposes of the history curriculum, then, was the pupil and the world which the pupil inhabits.

9　What is the future of the past?

In this final chapter, we will try to draw the threads of the book together, describing the conclusions we draw about the practice and thinking of history teachers, and the implications of our work for the development of the discipline and history teachers' professional understandings. We present our conclusions under five headings: history teachers' views of their practice and the school curriculum; the coherence of the history curriculum; the aims and goals of history teaching; the language and concepts in history teaching and communicating curriculum goals in history.

History teachers' views of their practice and the school curriculum

The first conclusion of significance relates to a striking contrast in our data. Almost without exception the teachers we worked with were upbeat about their classroom experience and their work in lessons. On the other hand, almost all were pessimistic about the future of history in the curriculum as a whole. In their lessons we observed highly skilled and sophisticated curriculum practitioners at work, and in their discussions of lessons we listened to teachers who clearly enjoyed their work with young people. They were exceptionally positive about their classroom practice and the strategies they were employing to improve the quality of young people's learning and achievement. A remarkable similarity emerged from our teachers: all talked about their positive engagement with the teaching of history and their own positive motivation to develop their professional practice. This conclusion is consistent with inspection evidence from Ofsted, who concluded in their 2001 survey of secondary subject teaching that:

> History teaching compares favourably with almost all other subjects. Many history teachers do their utmost to make lessons interesting

and significant, drawing on an impressive armoury of strategies. Stimulating introductions are followed by persistent and well-targeted questioning to elicit a developed response and stimulate curiosity.

(Ofsted 2001: 3)

Indeed, Her Majesty's Chief Inspector of Schools, reporting in 2002, identified history at Key Stage 4 as the best taught subject in schools (Ofsted 2002).

Remarkably, we found our teachers describing relatively few constraints on their professional practice. Some of the things which we had expected them to describe as constraints were not presented as such. The national curriculum, for example, was not seen as a constraint on practice; rather it was either simply accepted as part of the taken for granted professional landscape or, more positively, seen as a resource to be deployed in supporting pupil learning. Features of their pupils which we had expected the teachers to see as a constraint on their work – for example, low levels of literacy among some learners or negative attitudes to learning – were not seen as significant constraints but as planning issues which could be addressed through appropriate teaching strategies. In neither the lessons we observed nor the discussions about the curriculum was ICT used routinely, but difficulties about using ICT were not referred to as constraints. Perhaps most surprising of all, our teachers did not describe the lack of teaching time as a significant constraint; although we did not explicitly invite them to do so, they did not volunteer this as a factor in inhibiting their practice.

By contrast, even teachers in the most strikingly successful departments where examination results far outstripped those in the school more generally, were pessimistic about the long-term future of history in schools. They saw the subject increasingly on the defensive, under pressure from strategic curriculum interventions such as vocational courses or shifting curriculum priorities at a whole school level. In interview, our teachers saw the development of specialist schools, and the curriculum changes which followed specialist status, as a threat to the development of history in the school. More generally, as they perceived national educational priorities becoming increasingly concerned with instrumental outcomes, they felt that the policy climate was unsupportive of the place of history in the curriculum. There is, at least, an ironic contradiction between the inspection evidence on the quality of history teaching and our teachers' own positive engagement with classroom teaching on the one hand, and the rather bleaker views they expressed about the future of their subject.

The coherence of the history curriculum

A second set of conclusions relates to the issue of coherence at the level of single lessons, sequences of lessons and the curriculum as a whole. This sense of coherence was strong in a number of ways. Taking single lessons first, our teachers had a very strong, often highly intellectualized, sense of why particular activities had been planned, fitted together and related to objectives. Taking sequences of lessons, our teachers were able to explain clearly and convincingly why lessons were positioned as they were within given topics and why topics were positioned as they were within key stages. This was based on a model of the history curriculum which was intended to achieve particular outcomes. The history curriculum in our study schools had a strong coherence as a whole. This coherence manifested itself in a number of ways. Within each key stage teachers were able to explain the way in which content, ideas and activities had been planned in ways that enabled them to make meaningful links across and between individual units of work. Beyond this, the teachers we worked with understood and could articulate the ways in which work in one key stage could lay the foundations for work in the next. This highly coherent, clearly articulated and intellectually highly refined approach seemed to us to be more than mere curriculum planning and certainly more than the implementation of external guidelines. A way of expressing this is to describe it as the 'meta-curriculum': the underlying framework, highly integrated in terms of coherence, which drives the taught curriculum, and which was strongly thought through by teachers in spite of the external curriculum specifications which they were required to teach. The ways in which history teachers construct and organize the curriculum seems to us to depend in many crucial respects on this 'meta-curriculum'.

In discussing their departmental curricula, teachers constantly referred to curriculum issues in terms of their interrelationship, moving between what they had done, what they were doing and what they intended to do with high levels of sophistication. There was a difference in emphasis between the way teachers talked about curriculum issues in individual lessons and the way they talked about the history curriculum as a whole. It was striking that in discussing individual lessons our teachers' concern with history-specific goals was especially strong. In discussing the curriculum as a whole teachers talked in more general terms about the generic dimensions of the history curriculum. Looking back on this apparent discrepancy it becomes clear to us that at the curriculum level the history-specific aims were not so much missing as taken for granted: already assumed and already internalized. Our teachers were curriculum practitioners, and developers of high creativity and enormous skill. In some respects, indeed, this sense of coherence put teachers considerably ahead of examination specifications in terms of their thinking. An example relates to the use of source material in lessons, a key component of what we described as the 'alternative tradition' of history teaching. Through their Key Stage 3 teaching, where much innovation has taken place in evidential work, our teachers' expertise in this respect has outstripped the assumptions underpinning the demands of GCSE. Once again this demonstrates teachers' ability to think creatively about the relationship between what pupils are capable of achieving in lessons and the external demands on them.

The aims and goals of history teaching

A third set of conclusions relates to the aims and goals of history teaching. We saw in Chapters 1 and 2 that the goals of history teaching have frequently been highly contested and often contradictory. A striking outcome of our research was the *lack of tension* between what many commentators see as potentially competing goals. The teachers in our study had the professional grounding and intellectual confidence to integrate possible tensions between short-term knowledge acquisition and longer-term attitudinal development into a coherent set of intended outcomes for the subject. This was particularly the case in terms of what John Slater (1988) characterizes as the 'extrinsic' purposes of the subject. The teachers in our study were able to articulate a very clear and strong view of the unique contribution of history to young people's social education – in particular to their moral and political development. Sarah and Keith, for example, had a firm commitment to seeing history as an explicit vehicle for education in citizenship. Other teachers were more tentative, seeing citizenship education as a beneficial by-product of history teaching, but none of our teachers saw the purposes of history teaching as simply being intrinsic to the subject. While it is clear that the explicit political education components of citizenship, and the participatory citizenship components, cannot be taught through history curricula, it is clear that history is a flexible and malleable school subject, able to adapt and respond to changing demands. Here again, programmes of curriculum development and reform too often see subjects as being relatively stable and difficult to develop. Our conclusions suggest that the reverse may be true.

Language and concepts in history teaching

The fourth set of conclusions relates to the language of history teachers and the language of research in history education. It struck us that there are considerable gaps between these professional discourses, but also within them. At the most basic level, it is clear to us that history teachers discuss readily and with great confidence the 'skills' and 'concepts' their lessons and curricula are intended to develop. However, it is equally clear that there is little professional consensus on what the terms mean. Some teachers refer to 'concepts' to describe attributes which others refer to as 'skills' and vice versa: words are used to mean quite different things at different times. For example, 'causation' was often referred to as a skill rather than a concept. It is tempting to see this as a failure of teachers to understand the underlying concepts of their subject, but it would be quite wrong to do so, since it is also clear that within the history education research literature there is a lack of clarity about the use and meaning of key terms. In too many cases, individual researchers or schools of researchers coin neologisms which are not refined in dialogue with terms and ideas developed by other researchers or traditions. For example, researchers have used the labels 'substantive and procedural', 'first order and second order concepts' and 'knowing that and knowing how' to describe, in different ways, the same underlying ideas (Wineburg and Wilson 1991; Lee 1998; Lee and Ashby 2000). The consequence is that in too many cases professional discourse is relatively confused and confusing – perhaps especially so for novices. In order to harness the intellectual and professional energy we have located in curriculum construction and lesson planning, one of two things appears to be necessary. Either it is necessary to develop a far more coherent and consistent language for professional discourse, grounded in the ways in which professionals think about underlying concepts in practice, or it is necessary to accept – and recognize – some degree of latitude in the ways in which history in schools is described and discussed. The former seems to us to be a counsel of perfection; the latter accepts that the concepts and practice of classrooms frequently reflect the complexity and energy of real classroom life.

Communicating curriculum goals in history

A fifth set of conclusions relates to the communication of curriculum goals in the classroom. We have already noted the clarity with which teachers articulated their goals for the history curriculum and the sophistication of their understanding of the learning goals for lessons and parts of lessons. However, it was striking how rarely these goals were communicated explicitly to pupils or, when they were communicated, how it was done in a way which made it easy for pupils to miss them. This strikes us as worthy of comment in a number of respects. Most obviously, an enormous amount has been written on the significance of learning goals or teaching objectives in studies of classroom teaching. The research evidence we have suggests that clarity of learning goals is of critical importance in shaping effective pupil learning. Such is the emphasis on this that official guidance, in terms of inspection methodologies from Ofsted and explicit instruction in the Key Stage 3

Strategy, has stressed the importance of sharing learning goals with learners at the beginning of lessons. Were the teachers in our study being forgetful? This seems unlikely: the issue was not that they lacked clear goals but that they often chose not to make them explicit at the beginning of lessons. Something more complex was happening in relation to goals. What appears to have been happening in most lessons was that the goals, explicit at the planning stage, were made *implicitly* rather than explicitly clear to learners, and they were made implicitly clear through the ways in which lessons were constructed and activities presented. In terms of the discipline of history – which has been described as 'a good story well told' – the goals were being constructed through the materials and learning in the lessons. In too many cases, an explicit statement of goals at the beginning of the lesson would have, so to speak, given the ending away, or would have made what was a tentative and provisional conclusion about why Hitler came to power, or how the legend of Robin Hood has been presented, or Mao's motives on the Long March, too clear cut, and would have closed down, rather than opened out learning possibilities. Here as elsewhere, our teachers had a deeper, more sophisticated sense of the possibilities of knowledge *construction* in the classroom than curriculum specification and central directives would have allowed.

Conclusion

There are three further points on which to end this account. The first takes us back once more to Martin Booth's study of history teachers published in 1969. What is striking is the extent to which three decades of curriculum development, curriculum reform and teacher professional development have transformed the history classroom. We have few reservations in describing our teachers as more perceptive about their pupils, more informed about their discipline, more skilled in their practice and more sophisticated in their thinking than Booth's study group in the 1960s. That seems to us to be a cause for celebration, and we are happy to end our book by celebrating the richness of the work done in the classrooms in which we were privileged to work. The second relates to Kenneth Ruthven's arguments about 'warranted practice' in mathematics teaching (Ruthven 1999). We find Ruthven's work and its implications lucid and persuasive. It seems to us, on the basis of this study, that too little research and development in history education can be described as validated by 'warranted' accounts of professional practice. Our study has only scratched the surface of history teachers' thinking and practice, but it has done so sufficiently for us to be able to argue that it is possible to construct much richer and more securely grounded accounts of history teachers' work, planning and thinking, and so, by implication, of pupils' learning in history than we currently have. Our plea – to both practitioners and researchers –

would be to develop approaches to research and to developing history teaching which are genuinely 'warranted' through close engagement with what history teachers currently do. Our final point follows from these two and relates to curriculum and professional development. Our study has shown the complexity, richness and sophistication of history teachers' thinking and the skill, sensitivity and range of their practice. It follows from this that attempts to develop, extend and improve classroom practice need to take seriously the detailed professional knowledge which history teachers already possess and deploy. Programmes of curriculum reform, and the supporting professional development, which do not do this will simply fail because they do not appreciate the complexity already being actively managed by history teachers. Generic professional development, grounded on deficit model perceptions of what teachers are 'failing' to do, are unlikely to build on the things which are being done with great skill and sophistication. Worse, for those promoting change, if the professional development fails, the curriculum reform it supports will founder. What this study demonstrates is that history teachers have the knowledge and skill to implement reform programmes of great sophistication; equally, they have the knowledge and skill – perhaps fortunately – to thwart ill-conceived innovation. This knowledge and skill is something to be celebrated, certainly, but successful professional and curriculum development needs to understand and take account of it if significant development is to succeed.

APPENDIX

Appendix
Research methodology for the study reported in Sections 2 and 3

1 Research design

The research strategy chosen for the exploration was that of a multiple case study. 'Case study' here is intended to mean 'a strategy for doing research which involves an empirical investigation of a particular contemporary phenomenon within its real life context using multiple sources of evidence' (Robson 1993: 52), and one where the concern is with the 'situation (or phenomenon) as a whole' (Stenhouse 1978: 24). The appropriateness of this strategy was that it 'offers a means of investigating complex social units consisting of multiple variables of potential importance in understanding the phenomenon ... [and that] anchored in real life situations the case study results in a rich and holistic account of a phenomenon' (Merriam 1988: 32). We wanted to create a picture of the actual curriculum choices and classroom practices (the phenomenon explored) of a sample of practitioners, and in so doing understand something about both what these practitioners were doing but also why: what were their intentions and what factors helped or hindered them in achieving these intentions. Hence the strategy suited not only our research intentions, to understand the complex realities of the nature and interrelationships between beliefs and practice, but also our intended outcomes from the research: publications aimed at professional audiences who would value accessible descriptions and analyses of practice rooted in specific situations (Stenhouse 1985).

As Yin (1994) observes, a concern with case study methodology is its capacity for generalization. We do not claim to generalize from our selection of cases (see below) to all history departments – to an entire population – but instead we did anticipate using the multiple cases to generate 'theoretical propositions' (Yin 1994: 10). Our intention was that our case studies and cross-case comparisons generated from within these cases would 'produce a coherent and illuminating description of and perspective on a situation that is based on and consistent with detailed study of that situation'

(Ward Schofield 1993: 202), that is, the teaching of history within the chosen departments.

A key consideration within the research design was our choice of schools – how we selected our sample. The approach adopted was a modified system of purposive sampling. Purposive sampling 'offers the opportunity to learn' (Stake 1994: 243) and 'potential for learning is a different and sometimes superior criterion to representativeness. Balance and variety are important; the opportunity to learn is of primary importance' (Stake 1994: 234). Hence we chose to work with eight heads of history departments in a range of different schools. The schools varied in the following respects: their intake (gender, levels of attainment at entry, socio-economic indicators, levels of attainment at GCSE and post-16), their age ranges (11–18, 11–16, 13–18) and there was some variation in types of location (urban, small town and rural). The departments varied in terms of their stability, degree of development and composition (the number, experience and other responsibilities of the history teachers within the department). The heads of department varied in terms of their years of experience as teachers and as heads of department. Two characteristics common to all were that the head of department was keen to work with us and known to one of the researchers. This factor of familiarity was evidently valuable in terms of convenience but also enhanced opportunities to learn, given that only a limited amount of time could be devoted to the fieldwork and hence potentially lengthy familiarization procedures were not practicable.

The choice of relatively diverse school and departmental contexts was a deliberate decision: we were interested to explore the commonalities and differences that would emerge from heads of departments working in very different contexts, and if it would be possible to attribute any of these to contextual factors.

To achieve the overall aim of the research and to provide direction to the processes of data collection and especially analysis, the following specific research questions were formulated:

i   What curriculum choices have been made by the heads of department and why?
ii   What sorts of activities are enacted in observed history lessons and why?
iii   What sort of future does the head of department see for the place of history in the curriculum in the future (a) within his or her own school and (b) more generally?
iv   What appear to be the dominant concerns of the head of department about the history curriculum as a whole (drawing on the analysis for questions i and iii)?
v   What appear to be the dominant concerns of the head of department,

about the enactment of the history curriculum as a whole (drawing on the analysis for question ii)?

vi   What are the similarities and differences between his or her concerns for the curriculum as a whole and its enactment in the classroom (drawing on the analysis from questions iv and v)?

vii What are the similarities and differences in the concerns of the heads of department?

viii What can be elucidated to explain these similarities and differences?

2 Research strategy

2.1 Data collection methods

Several principles guided our choice of methods of data collection and our choices were informed by the type of strategy first adopted by Brown and McIntyre (1993) and subsequently by Cooper and McIntyre (1996), with an emphasis on the positive, a focus on shared experiences, an open approach in interviews and by overtly helping teachers gain access to the required information. Although these principles needed to be adapted to accommodate our concerns – which went beyond classroom practice – they nonetheless suggest the spirit of our methods. First and foremost they needed to generate valid data that would enable us to address the issues of interest; this was a key consideration in terms of the choice of the specific methods and in the range of methods of data collection employed. Hence, for example, we chose to observe and then interview teachers about observed practice (rather than just interviewing about practice) so that the interviews would be rooted in the shared experience of practice and hence maximize the authenticity and validity of that data. Second, they needed to be methods that were acceptable to the teachers involved: they must be economic in terms of the teachers' time, make relatively few professional or emotional demands on them, be seen to be positive about the teacher's expertise and be open to scrutiny by the teachers. Certain methods had to be discounted, most notably the use of stimulated recall using video or audio recording which, while potentially a very rich source in relation to practice, would be very time consuming, technically complex and potentially threatening to the teachers. Third, they needed to be methods that could be replicated across contexts and by several researchers; hence, any form of participant observation was similarly discounted. And finally they had to be economic and efficient in terms of the researcher's time.

In the light of these considerations, and some initial trialling, the following methods were used:

2.1.1 Classroom observation

Each head of department was observed teaching history for a series of lessons on the same day. The teacher chose the lessons to be observed and was asked to choose lessons with groups 'with whom they felt comfortable'. The intention here was to maximize opportunities for us to learn from the teachers in terms of their practice and our assumption was that we would be most successful in doing this if the teacher had full control over the choice. It was indicated in advance that we hoped to interview the teacher afterwards about one or two of the lessons, but if at any stage the teacher wanted to stop the observation or the subsequent interview, then they were free to do so. While recognizing that observers will inevitably affect the classroom dynamic, the role of the researcher here was that of non-participant observer with the intention of disrupting as little as possible the 'normal' classroom environment.

To give some shape to the observation a simple proforma was adopted. This recorded factual information concerning the school, the teacher, the year group, the band or set, the time and date of the lesson, the lesson topic and the title of any textbook(s) or resources used in the lesson. The substance of the record was a non-evaluative description, in note form, of what was happening in the lesson with particular attention paid to: teacher talk, the questions asked, the activities engaged in by the pupils and the resources used. Alongside this record, questions to raise in the subsequent interview were noted. These questions were principally concerned with clarifying what the teacher was doing at each point in the lesson and why they were doing that. Throughout, the focus was on the teaching and learning of history: issues of management, for example, were only explored in so far as they were directly related to the teaching and learning agenda of the teacher.

2.1.2 Interviews on classroom observation

Following the observations the teacher was interviewed about what had happened during each lesson, using the lesson observation record as a basis for the interview. The key concerns in this interview were with what the teacher was hoping to achieve at each stage of the lesson and why they were using the approaches observed. The interview was conducted as soon as possible after the observed lesson(s) so that the lesson would be fresh in the teacher's mind, and an emphasis was placed on making sense of the teacher's practice rather than in making judgements about it. The interviews varied in length, in part depending on the length and complexity of the lesson, but on average were 45–60 minutes long and were tape-recorded.

2.1.3 General interviews about the history curriculum

Each head of department was also interviewed about the nature of the history curriculum offered by their department. Our intention here was to explore their goals for history teaching in their school. Thus, for example, in relation to Key Stage 3 they were asked which study units they had chosen to teach and why they had chosen them. We also asked about what emphases they put and why. In relation to Key Stage 4 we asked which GCSE syllabus they had chosen and why. We asked what they thought it offered the pupils and what they hoped pupils would go away with from having done GCSE history. Similar questions were asked about AS history. In some instances the head of department had inherited choices from a predecessor and here we asked about why they had not made changes and in what ways they valued what they did offer.

We then moved on to ask their views about the nature and future of the history curriculum more generally. First we asked about its future within their own school: Were they optimistic? Why? Why not? Then we asked about the future of history in the school curriculum more generally. Again we probed if they were optimistic or not, and why. Our final question was speculative: we asked if there were any content areas that they would regard as absolutely essential components of a history curriculum.

These interviews were always scheduled after the lesson observations and associated interviews: we did not want what was said in these to have the potential to affect or distort the observed practice of the teachers. They normally lasted for an hour and were tape-recorded.

2.1.4 Departmental handbooks
To provide contextual information about the department and its practice each department was asked to give us a copy of their current departmental handbook. The handbook provided a range of evidence. It set out in greater detail the schemes of work which supported syllabi and study units but also provided a wide range of contextual data. Pupil performance data allowed the department to be set in the context of pupil entry and exit characteristics. Departmental policy statements provided a frame through which observed and described practice could be examined. The formal statement of departmental aims and objectives provided a view of departmental concerns.

2.1.5 Descriptive and statistical information about the school and the department
To provide contextual information, each head of department was asked to give us information on the following:

- Contextual information about the school, such as the nature of the catchment area, free school meals, GCSE/A level trends.
- Information about the department, that is, names of members of the department, and then, for each member, the amount of history taught (periods out of total), subjects other than history taught, number of years of teaching experience, years in this post,

responsibilities in the department, responsibilities in the school and their qualifications.

- Information about curriculum provision: approximate class sizes for history, timetable allocation for history, pupil grouping for each year group, if they were banded or setted and the basis for this.
- Assessment information and data: GCSE and A level history results for the previous year, information about any formal assessments done during Key Stage 3, any Key Stage 3 assessment data for last year.

2.2 Data analysis procedures

The approaches we adopted to data analysis were influenced by both a grounded theory approach (Glaser and Strauss 1967) and Wolcott's (1994) distinction between description, analysis and interpretation in the transformation of qualitative data. We wanted to be able to use our data to describe the actions and choices of the history teachers, both in the classroom and in the nature of the history curriculum. We wanted to be able to analyse both their intentions and the factors that may have helped or hindered them in carrying out these intentions. We wanted to be able to understand their hopes and fears for the future of the history curriculum, and ultimately we wanted to be able to interpret what we had discovered: to 'make sense of meaning in context . . . [to consider] What's to be made of it all?' (Miles and Huberman 1994: 14). Our intention was to build secure and comprehensive categories from our data, and through these to offer first an account of the individual heads of department and then to move beyond these individual cases to a cross-case comparison expressed in terms of theoretical propositions abstracted from the situated examples. We were conscious of having different types of data and the need to adopt procedures in relation to each that would be appropriate to the nature and status of the data, to relate closely to our focused research questions and to contribute to the sorts of accounts that we wished to create.

To achieve these aims, data sets were treated in the following ways:

2.2.1 Classroom observation data

Initially it had been intended that this data might be subjected to analytical procedures designed to explore the nature of the classroom strategies employed by the teacher. However, inspection of the data indicated that they were not sufficiently robust or detailed to support such an analysis and instead that they needed to be viewed as the means to collecting the interview data about the lesson. In consequence, these data were used only to write a brief description of the observed lesson that could then be used to contextualize the findings from the interviews.

2.2.2 Interviews on classroom observation

This data was first transcribed. After repeated reading of the transcriptions to achieve familiarization with the data, a set of procedures for analysis were developed and tested out independently by the researchers. The aim of these procedures was to identify the teacher's intentions in the lesson and factors impinging on these intentions. These two key categories emerged from the specific research questions and the data itself. Initially, the foci for analysis were 'reasons for' and 'factors influencing' but initial attempts at analysis suggested that it was often difficult to distinguish between the action itself and the reasons for it, and given the focus of the interview questions – always seeking to probe why the teacher had done certain things and what they were trying to achieve – it became apparent that intentions and impinging factors were the most appropriate categories to make sense of what the teacher had said in the interview, in the terms of interest to the research.

The first stage in the procedure was to go through the transcript, high-lighting all examples of intentions expressed by the teacher. These were identified, from the teacher's use of language, as statements concerned with what he or she intended to happen or be achieved in the lesson. Phrases such as 'I want them to', 'get them to look at', 'make them think', 'I was aiming to', 'the point was', all exemplify how we identified such intentions.

The second stage involved highlighting everything identified as affecting the teacher's intentions in some way, such as the nature and complexity of the history being studied (for example, 'some of the reasons are quite complex so I . . .'), nature of the school intake (for example, 'literacy is an issue . . . it's the same for the majority of our boys'), the nature of the group (for example, 'this group is a really lively lot so . . .'), the resources available (for example, the cartoons we have for that . . . they show it up in quite a straightforward way'), and so on.

The third stage involved reviewing the transcript and any unmarked text to see if the first two stages had been comprehensive or if further intentions or impinging factors (or talk related to these such as statements leading up to the expression of intention or further elaboration of an intention or factor) could be identified.

The fourth stage involved reviewing the transcript to see if there were any sections of teacher talk that were not amenable to classification as intention or impinging factor. In the event, the categories of intentions and impinging factors did account for most of the data. Statements that did not fit into these categories were identified as being of two types (i) general contextual state-ments about the school, class, department or curriculum where no direct link was made by the teacher to the intentions in the lesson, for example, 'generally the [Ofsted] report was very good but they said we're not doing enough to raise literacy'; (ii) generalized statements of the teacher's beliefs or philosophy, again not directly related to the observed lesson, for example,

'I'm really happy we don't have tiered papers [at GCSE] ... my whole philosophy is differentiation by outcome.'

The next stage involved listing, in the teacher's own words, all the intentions expressed, and, separately, all the impinging factors, to see if each of these broad categories could be subdivided and hence individual intentions or factors grouped in some way. The intention here was to move beyond the teacher's own words and begin to conceptualize what they were talking about in a way abstracted from the original data. Groupings were formed by considering what it was that the teacher had been referring to and the ways in which it might be similar to another utterance. Hence here we began to see the emergence of certain dominant themes or concerns in the teacher's thinking and practice. In the case of one teacher, for example, many of his intentions related to the sorts of historical understandings he wanted the pupils to develop ('to see why Hitler came to power', 'to empathise with what the German people were faced with', 'wanted them to understand the Nazi approach to it', 'to see it [Nazi propaganda] as something which at the time was actually very new and different'), while for another, achieving pupil engagement was an important idea common to a number of his statements of intent ('I do some standard ones [question and answer sessions] but at other times I'm always trying to think, what is motivating the pupils?', 'I want them to have reasons to think about it and try to find an answer', 'I wanted them to get interested in it so what we did . . .', 'I think they're really gripped . . . by powerful examples'). In the case of impinging factors, the nature and demands of GCSE examinations was identified as linking several statements (for several of the teachers), while another factor for one teacher was that of the pupils' skills.

These procedures thus led to the creation, for each of the teachers, of a picture of their dominant concerns for this lesson, in relation to their intentions and the factors impinging on these. In addition, certain aspects of contextual information had been identified and areas of belief or philosophy not directly related to the teaching of this lesson.

Once we had established pictures of the lessons in terms of the teachers' intentions and impinging factors, patterns appeared within these fruitful avenues for further analysis. A specific issue that emerged both from our data and the existing literature on teacher expertise was the types of knowledge that teachers hold. Hence the lesson interview data were then re-analysed, following procedures similar to those employed in the first take on the data, in terms of their subject knowledge, their knowledge about their pupils and their knowledge about resources and activities. Segments of data which revealed most clearly the interactions between these types of knowledge were subjected to especially close scrutiny to explore the ways in which teachers' goals, the activities for lessons and their thinking about progression reflected their deployment of the different types.

2.2.3 General interviews about the history curriculum

The data related to curriculum choices (that is, the responses to the first three questions) were analysed using exactly the same procedures as those used for the lesson observation interviews. The intention here was again to generate a picture of dominant concerns at the level of the curriculum, so that these concerns could be compared and contrasted with those generated at the level of specific lessons.

In terms of the interview questions concerned with the future of the history curriculum, two questions guided the analysis: is the teacher negative or positive about the future? What reasons are expressed for this view? Once reasons for the view had been identified, these were listed and, where possible, categorized in a way similar to the procedures used for the other interview data. For the final question, concerned with the teacher's ideas for curriculum content, what we were most interested to discover was the teacher's rationale for their position, so again we isolated these elements of their talk and looked for patterns or linking ideas to make sense of their thinking. To do this we referred back to the dominant concerns identified at the lesson and curriculum levels to see if we could identify any continuities or discontinuities in their beliefs.

2.2.4 Documentary analysis of departmental handbooks and additional information provided by the school

The intention in collecting the handbooks was to provide us with additional contextual information about the schools and the history departments and also to act as a form of triangulation in relation to statements made by teachers in their interviews. In the event, it proved inappropriate and impossible to attempt any systematic analysis of these documents since they varied in so many respects. Some were very lengthy, others very short, their formats varied considerably, some were clearly working documents, others were produced primarily for Ofsted inspection purposes and it was evident that some were already out of date. Although these differences are in themselves a matter of interest, and it may be the case that our findings make reference to these varying features of the departmental documentation, primarily they have been used in a descriptive fashion to enable us to create a picture of the context within which each teacher is working. The additional information collected from each of the schools has been treated in a similar fashion and was designed specifically for this purpose.

The final stage in the analysis moved from the individual cases to a cross-case comparison. Here the findings from each case were considered in relation to two key questions: What were the similarities and differences in the concerns of the heads of department? What might explain these similarities and differences? While the analysis at the level of individual cases deliberately sought to understand each teacher's thinking and practice in their own terms (and hence each was analysed independently of the others), here the analysis was significantly abstracted from the original data and was dependent on first the researchers' interpretations of the ways in which concerns were similar (even if expressed in varying ways) or different, and second the researchers' identification of possible reasons for these similarities and differences.

Bibliography

Alexander, R. (1996) *Policy and Practice in Primary Education: Local Initiative, National Agenda*, 2nd edn. London: Routledge.

Andreetti, K. (1993) *Teaching History from Primary Evidence*. London: David Fulton.

Arthur, J. and Phillips, R. (eds) (2000) *Issues in History Teaching*. London: Routledge.

Arthur, J., Davies, I., Wrenn, A., Haydn, T. and Kerr, D. (2001) *Citizenship Through Secondary History*. London: Routledge Falmer.

Ashby, R., Lee, P.J. and Dickinson, A.K. (1995) Progression in children's ideas about history, in M. Hughes (ed.) *Progression in Learning* (BERA Dialogue) Clevedon: Multilingual Matters.

Ashby, R., Lee, P.J. and Dickinson, A.K. (1996) 'There were no facts in those days': children's ideas about historical explanation, in M. Hughes (ed.) *Teaching and Learning in Changing Times*. Oxford: Basil Blackwell.

Ashby, R., Lee, P.J. and Dickinson, A.K. (1997) Just another emperor: understanding action in the past, *International Journal of Education Research*, 27(3):233–44.

Askew, M. and Wiliam, D. (1995) *Recent Research in Mathematics Education: 5–16*. London: HSMO.

Bage, G. (1999) *Narrative Matters: Teaching and Learning History through Story*. London: Falmer.

Bage, G. (2000) *Thinking History 4–14: Teaching, Learning, Curricula and Communities*. London: Routledge Falmer.

Ball, S. (1992) Subject departments and the 'implementation' of national curriculum policy: an overview of the issues, *Journal of Curriculum Studies*, 24(2): 97–115.

Banham, D. (1998) Getting ready for the grand prix: learning how to build a substantiated argument in Year 7, *Teaching History*, 92: 6–15.

Banham, D. with Culpin, C. (2002) Ensuring progression continues into GCSE: let's not do for our pupils with our plan of attack, *Teaching History*, 108: 16–22.

Barker, B. (2002) Values and practice: history teaching 1971–2001, *Cambridge Journal of Education*, 32(1): 61–72.

Barton, K. (2001) 'You'd be wanting to know about the past': social contexts of children's understanding in Northern Ireland and the USA, *Comparative Education*, 37(1): 89–106.

Black, P. and Wiliam, D. (1998) Assessment and classroom learning, *Assessment in Education*, 5: 7–74.

Blyth, W.A.L. (1975) *History, Geography and Social Science 8–13: An Introduction*. London: Collins.

Booth, M.B. (1969) *History Betrayed?* Longman: Harlow.

Booth, M. (1979) A longitudinal study of cognitive skills, concepts and attitudes of adolescents studying a modern world history syllabus and an analysis of their adductive historical thinking. Unpublished PhD thesis, Reading University.

Booth, M. (1987) Ages and concepts: a critique of the Piagetian approach to history teaching, in C. Portal (ed.) *The History Curriculum for Teachers*. Lewes: Falmer.

Bousted, M. and Davies, I. (1996) Teachers' perceptions of models of political learning. *Curriculum*, 17(1): 12–23.

Brophy, J. and Van Sledright, B. (1997) *Teaching and Learning History in Elementary Schools*. New York: Teachers' College Press.

Brown, S. and McIntyre, D. (1993) *Making Sense of Teaching*. Buckingham: Open University Press.

Bullough, R.V. (2001) Pedagogical content knowledge circa 1907 and 1987: a study in the history of an idea, *Teaching and Teacher Education*, 17: 655–66.

Burke, P. (ed.) (2001) *New Perspectives on Historical Writing*, 2nd edn. Cambridge: Polity Press.

Busher, H. and Harris, A. (1999) Leadership of school subject areas: tensions and dilemmas of managing in the middle, *School Leadership and Management*, 19(3): 305–17.

Byrom, J., Counsell, C. and Riley, M. (1997) *Think Through History: Medieval Minds*. London: Longman.

Calderhead, J. (1984) *Teachers' Classroom Decision-making*. London: Holt, Rinehart and Winston.

Carter, K. (1990) Teachers' knowledge and learning to teach, in W.R. Houston (ed) *Handbook of Research on Teacher Education*. New York: Macmillan.

Cercadillo, L. (1998) Significance in history: students ideas in England and Spain. Unpublished PhD thesis, University of London.

Chancellor, V. (1970) *History for their Masters: History in the School Textbook, 1800–1914*. London: Penguin.

Chitty, C. (2002) *Understanding Schools and Schooling*. London: Routledge Falmer.

Clarke, J. and Wrigley, K. (1991) *Special Needs in Ordinary Schools: Humanities for All*. London: Cassell.

Cockcroft, W.H. (1982) *Mathematics Counts*. London: HMSO.

Coltham, J.B. and Fines, J. (1970) *Educational Objectives for the Study of History*. London: The Historical Association.

Cooper, P. and McIntyre, D. (1996) *Effective Teaching and Learning: Teachers' and Students' Perspectives*. Buckingham: Open University Press.

Counsell, C. (1997) *Analytical and Discursive Writing at Key Stage 3*. London: The Historical Association.

Counsell, C. (2000a) Didn't we do that in Year 7? Planning for progress in evidential understanding, *Teaching History*, 99: 36–41.

Counsell, C. (2000b) Historical knowledge and historical skills: a distracting dichotomy, in J. Arthur and R. Phillips (eds) *Issues in History Teaching*. London: Routledge.

Counsell, C. and the Historical Association Secondary Education Committee (1997) *Planning the Twentieth Century World*. London: The Historical Association.

Crick, B. (1998) *Education for Citizenship and the Teaching of Democracy in Schools: Final Report of the Advisory Committee on Citizenship*. London: Qualifications and Curriculum Authority.

Crick, B. and Porter, A. (eds) (1978) *Political Education and Political Literacy*. London: Longman.

Cunningham, D. (2001) Expertise in the teaching of historical empathy. Unpublished paper presented at University of Oxford Research Seminar, 28 September.

Cunningham, D. (2002) Tailoring existing analytical concepts to a study about teaching historical empathy. Unpublished paper presented at British Educational Research Association Conference, 10 September.

Davies, I. (2001) Citizenship and the teaching and learning of history, in J. Arthur and R. Phillips (eds) *Issues in History Teaching*. London: Routledge.

DES (Department of Education and Science) (1988) *Education Reform Act*. London: HMSO.

DES (Department of Education and Science) (1990) *History in the National Curriculum: Final Report of the History Working Group*. London: HMSO.

DfEE QCA (1999) The National Curriculum for England: History Key Stages 1–3. London: QCA.

DfEE (2000) http://www.dfes.gov.uk/statistics/DB/VOL/vø192/index.html (accessed 1 April 2003).

Dickinson, A.K. and Lee, P.J. (1994) Investigating progression in children's ideas about history: the CHATA Project, in P. John and P. Lucas (eds) *Partnership and Progress*. Sheffield: SCHTE in association with the Division of Education, University of Sheffield.

Dickinson, A.K., Gard, A. and Lee, P.J. (1978) Evidence in history and the classroom, in A.K. Dickinson and P.J. Lee (eds) *History Teaching and Historical Understanding*. London: Heinemann.

Dilek, D. (1998) History in the Turkish elementary school: perceptions and pedagogy. Unpublished PhD thesis, University of Warwick.

Earley, P. *et al.* (1998) *School Improvement After Inspection? School and LEA Responses*. London: Paul Chapman (in association with the British Educational Management and Administration Society).

Edwards, A.D. (1978) The 'language of history' and the communication of historical knowledge, in A.K. Dickinson and P.J. Lee (eds) *History Teaching and Historical Understanding*. London: Heinemann.

Elliott, J. (1989) Education in the shadow of the education reform act. First Lawrence Stenhouse Memorial Lecture, University of East Anglia.

Elton, G.R. (1969) *The Practice of History*. Glasgow: Collins Fontana.

Farmer, A. and Knight, P. (1995) *Active History in Key Stages 3 and 4*. London: David Fulton.

Feiman-Nemser, S. and Remillard, J. (1995) *Perspectives on Learning to Teach*. Lansing, MI: National Centre for Research on Teacher Learning, Michigan State University (Issues Papers).

Fenstermacher, G.D. (1994) The knower and the known: the nature of knowledge in research on teaching, in L. Darling-Hammond (ed.) *Review of Research in Education*, 20: 3–56.

Ferro, M. (1984) *The Use and Abuse of History: How the Past is Taught*. London: Routledge and Kegan Paul.

Fogelman, K.R. (1991) *Citizenship in Schools*. London: Fulton.

Furlong, T., Venkatakrishnan, H. and Brown, M. (2000) *Key Stage 3 National Strategy: An Evaluation of the Strategies for Literacy and Mathematics*. London: Association of Teachers and Lecturers.

Galton, M., Gray, J. and Rudduck, J. (1999) *The Impact of School Transitions and Transfers on Pupil Progress and Attainment*. London: DfEE.

Glaser, B.G. and Strauss, A.L. (1967) *The Discovery of Grounded Theory: Strategies for Qualitative Research*. Chicago: Aldine.

Gorman, M. (1998) The 'structured enquiry' is not a contradiction in terms: focused teaching for independent learning. *Teaching History* 92: 20–5.

Grossman, P. (2002) Teacher Knowledge and Professional Education: The Case of Pedagogical Content Knowledge. Unpublished paper, Key Note Address, Inaugural UPSO International Teacher Education Conference, Kuala Lumpur, 6 May.

Grosvenor, I. (2000) 'History for the nation' multiculturalism and the teaching of history, in J. Arthur and R. Phillips (eds) *Issues in History Teaching*. London: Routledge.

Gudmundsdottir, S. (1991) Pedagogical models of subject matter, in J. Brophy (ed.) *Advances in Research on Teaching Vol. 2*. Greenwich: JAI Press.

Gudmundsdottir, S. and Shulman, L. (1989) Pedagogical knowledge in social studies, in J. Lowyck and C.M. Clark (eds) *Teacher Thinking and Professional Action*. Leuven: Leuven University Press.

Hallam, R.N. (1975) A study of the effect of teaching method on the growth of logical thought with special reference to the teaching of history using criteria from Piaget's theory of cognitive development. Unpublished PhD thesis, University of Leeds.

Halliday, F. (2002) *Two Hours that Shook the World: September 11 2001, Causes and Consequences*. London: Routledge.

Harris, A. (1999) *Effective Subject Departments*. London: David Fulton.

Haydn, T. (2000) Information and communications technology in the history classroom, in J. Arthur and R. Phillips (eds) *Issues in History Teaching*. London: Routledge.

Helsby, G. (1999) *Changing Teachers' Work: The 'Reform' of Secondary Schooling*. Buckingham: Open University Press.

HMI (Her Majesty's Inspector) (1985) *History in the Primary and Secondary Years*. London: HMSO.

Hobsbawm, E. J. (1969) *Bandits*. London: Weidenfeld & Nicolson.

Hsaio, Y.M. (2002) Exploring students' ideas about historical accounts in textbooks. Unpublished MA dissertation, University of London Institute of Education.

Hunt, M. (2000) Teaching historical significance, in J. Arthur and R. Phillips (eds) *Issues in History Teaching*. London: Routledge.

Husbands, C. (1996) *What is History Teaching?: Language, Ideas and Meaning in Learning about the Past*. Buckingham: Open University Press.

Husbands, C. (2001) What's happening in history? Trends in GCSE and 'A' Level examinations, 1993–2000, *Teaching History*, 103: 37–41.

Husbands, C. and Pendry, A. (2000) Research and practice in history teacher education, *Cambridge Journal of Education*, 30(3): 321–34.

Inhelder, B. and Piaget, J. (1958) *The Growth of Logical Thinking from Childhood to Adolescence*. London: Routledge and Kegan Paul.

Ireson, J., Mortimore, P. and Hallam, S. (2002) What do we know about effective pedagogy? in B. Moon, A. Shelton Mayes and S. Hutchinson (eds) *Teaching, Learning and the Curriculum in Secondary Schools*. London: Routledge Falmer.

Jenkins, K. (1991) *Rethinking History*. London: Routledge.

Keatinge, M.W. (1910) *Studies in the Teaching of History* London: A & C Black.

Kinloch, N. (1998) Learning about the Holocaust: moral or historical question? *Teaching History*, 93: 44–6.

Kundera, M. (1982) *The Book of Laughter and Forgetting*. London: Faber and Faber.

Labbett, B.D.C. (1979) Towards a curriculum specification for history, *Journal of Curriculum Studies*, 11(2): 125–37.

Labbett, B.D.C. (1996) *Personal Principles of Procedure and the Expert Teacher*, http://www.uea.ac.uk/care/elu/Issues/Education/Ed4.html.

Lee, P.J. (1991) Historical knowledge and the national curriculum, in R. Aldrich (ed) *History in the National Curriculum*. London: Kogan Page.

Lee, P.J. (1998) History education research in the UK: a schematic commentary. Unpublished paper, Curriculum Studies Group, University of London Institute of Education.

Lee, P.J. and Ashby, R. (1987) Children's concepts of empathy and understanding in history, in C. Portal (ed.) *The History Curriculum for Teachers*. Lewes: Falmer.

Lee, P.J. and Ashby, R. (2001) Progression in historical understanding among students ages 7–14, in P. Seixas, P. Stearns and S. Wineburg, (eds) *Teaching, Learning and Knowing History*. New York: New York University Press.

Levstik, L. (2000) Articulating the silences: teachers' and adolescents' conceptions of historical significance, in P.N. Stearns, P. Seixas and S. Wineburg (eds) *Knowing, Teaching and Learning History*. London: New York University Press.

Ma, L. (1999) *Knowing and Teaching Elementary Mathematics*. Mahwah, NJ: Lawrence Erlbaum and Associates.

McBer, H. (2000) *Research into Teacher Effectiveness: A Model of Teacher Effectiveness*. London: DfES.

MacGilchrist, B., Myers, K. and Reed, J. (1997) *The Intelligent School*. London: Paul Chapman Publishing.

McCutcheon, G. and Milner, H.R. (2002) A contemporary study of teacher planning in a high school English class, *Teachers and Teaching: Theory and Practice*, 8(1): 81–94.

McIntyre, D. (2002) Has classroom teaching served its day? in B. Moon, A. Shelton Mayes and S. Hutchinson (eds) *Teaching, Learning and the Curriculum in Secondary Schools*. London: RoutledgeFalmer.

McMahon, A. (2001) A cultural perspective of school effectiveness, school improvement and teacher professional development, in A. Harris and N. Bennett (eds) *School Effectiveness and School Improvement: Alternative Perspectives*. London: Continuum.

Merriam, S. (1988) *Case Study Research in Education: Qualitative Approach*. San Francisco: Jossey Bass Publishers.

Miles, M.B. and Huberman, A.M. (1994) *Qualitative Data Analysis*. London: Sage.

Morgan, C. and Morris, G. (1999) *Good Teaching: Pupils and Teachers Speak*. Buckingham: Open University Press.

Muijs, D. and Reynolds, D. (2001) *Effective Teaching: A Handbook of Evidence-based Methods*. London: Paul Chapman.

NCC (National Curriculum Council) (1990) *Education for Citizenship*. York: NCC.

Ofsted (2001) *Ofsted Subject Reports 1999/2000: History*. London: The Stationery Office.

Ofsted (2002) *The Annual Report of Her Majesty's Chief Inspector of Schools*. London: The Stationery Office.

Ogborn, K.J., Kress, G., Martins, I. and McGillicuddy, K. (1996) *Explaining Science in the Classroom*. Buckingham: Open University Press.

Pankhania, J. (1994) *Liberating the National History Curriculum*. London: Falmer.

Peel, E. (1960) *The Pupil's Thinking*. London: Oldbourne.

Peel, E. (1966) Some problems in the psychology of history teaching, in W.H. Burston and D. Thompson (eds) *Studies in the Nature and Teaching of History*. London: Routledge and Kegan Paul.

Pendry, A. (1994) The pre-lesson pedagogical decision making of history student teachers during the internship year. Unpublished DPhil thesis, University of Oxford.

Phillips, R. (1998) *History Teaching, Nationhood and the State: A Study in Educational Politics*. London: Cassell.

Phillips, R. (2000) Government policies, the state and the teaching of history, in J. Arthur and R. Phillips (eds) *Issues in History Teaching*. London: Routledge.

Phillips, R. (2002) *Reflective Teaching of History 11–18: Meeting Standards and Applying Research*. London: Continuum.

Price, M. (1968) History in danger, *History*, 53: 342–7.

Pring, R. (1995) The community of educated people. The Lawrence Stenhouse Memorial lecture, *British Journal of Educational Studies*, 43(2): 121–45.

Prins, G. (2002) *The Heart of War: On Power, Conflict and Obligation in the Twenty-first Century*. London: Routledge.

Putnam, C. (2002) Letter, *Teaching History*, 108: 7.

QCA (Qualifications and Curriculum Authority) (1998) *Education for Citizenship and the Teaching of Democracy in Schools. Part 1 : Advisory Group Initial Report*. London: QCA.

QCA (Qualifications and Curriculum Authority) (2000) *The National Curriculum for England: History*. London: Qualifications and Curriculum Authority.

Reeves, M. (1980) *Why History?* Harlow: Longman.

Riley, M. (1997) Big stories and big pictures: making overviews and outlines interesting, *Teaching History*, 88: 20–2.

Riley, M. (2000) Into the Key Stage 3 history garden: choosing and planting your enquiry questions, *Teaching History*, 99: 8–13.

Robson, C. (1993) *Real World Research*. Oxford: Blackwell Publishers.

Rogers, P. (1978) *The New History – Theory into Practice*. London: The Historical Association.

Rogers, P. (1984) The power of visual presentation, in A.K. Dickinson, P.J. Lee and P.J. Rogers (eds) *Learning History*. London: Heinemann.

Rowbotham, S. (1973) *Hidden from History: 300 Years of Women's Oppression and the Fight Against It*. London: Pluto Press.

Rudduck, J. and Flutter, J. (2000) Pupil participation and pupil perspective: carving a new order of experience, *Cambridge Journal of Education*, 30(1): 75–89.

Ruthven, K. (1999) Reconstructing professional judgement in mathematics education: from good practice to warranted practice, in C. Hoyles, C. Morgan and G. Woodhouse (eds) *Rethinking the Mathematics Curriculum*. London: Falmer.

Samuel, R. (1994) *Theatres of Memory. Vol. 1: Past and Present in Contemporary Culture*. London: Verso.

Schagen, S. and Kerr, D. (1999) *Bridging the Gap? The National Curriculum and Progression from Primary to Secondary School*. Slough: NFER.

Schools' Council (1976) *A New Look at History*. Edinburgh: Holmes McDougall.

Seixas, P. (1996) Conceptualising the growth of historical understanding, in D.R. Olson and N. Torrance (eds) *The Handbook of Education and Human Development*. Oxford: Blackwell.

Shemilt, D. (1980) *History 13–16 Evaluation Study*. Edinburgh: Holmes McDougall.

Shemilt, D. (1983) The devil's locomotive, *History and Theory*, 22(1): 1–18.

Shemilt, D. (1984) Beauty and the philosopher: empathy in history and the classroom, in A.K. Dickinson, P.J. Lee and P. Rogers (eds) *Learning History*. London: Heinemann.

Shemilt, D. (1987) Adolescent ideas about evidence and methodology in history, in C. Portal (ed.) *The History Curriculum for Teachers*. Lewes: Falmer.

Shephard, C. and Brown, B. (1996) *Discovering the Past: Britain 1750–1900 Teachers' Resource Book, Special Needs Support Materials*. London: John Murray.

Shephard, C. and Moore, A. (1997) *Discovering the Past: The Twentieth Century World Teachers' Resource Book, Special Needs Support Materials*. London: John Murray.

Shephard, C., Reid, A. and Shephard, K. (1993) *Discovering the Past: Peace and War*. London: John Murray.

Shulman, L.S. (1986) Those who understand: knowledge growth in teaching, *Educational Researcher*, 15(2): 4–14.

Slater, J. (1988) *The Politics of History Teaching: A Humanity Dehumanized?* Special Professorial Lecture. London: Institute of Education.

Slater, J. (1989) Where there is dogma, let us sow doubt, in J. White (ed.) *The Aims of Hadrian School History: The National Curriculum and Beyond*. London: University of London Institute of Education (Bedford Way Papers).

Slater, J. (1995) *Teaching History in the New Europe*. London: Cassell.

Slater, J. and Hennessey, R.A.S. (1978) Political competence, in B. Crick and A. Porter (eds) *Political Education and Political Literacy*. London: Longman.

Speaker's Commission (1990) *Encouraging Citizenship*. London: HMSO.

SREB (Southern Regional Examination Boad) (1986) *Empathy in History: From Definition to Assessment*. Basingstoke: SREB.

Stake, R.E. (1994) Case studies, in N.K. Denzin and Y.S. Lincoln (eds) *Handbook of Research on Education*. Thousand Acres, CA: Sage.

Stenhouse, L. (1968) The Humanities Curriculum Project, *Journal of Curriculum Studies*, 1 (1): 26–33.

Stenhouse, L. (1975) *An Introduction to Curriculum Research and Development*. London: Heinemann.

Stenhouse, L. (1978) Case study and case records: towards a contemporary history of education, *British Educational Research Journal*, 4 (2): 21–39.

Stenhouse, L. (1985) Using research means doing research, in J. Rudduck and D. Hopkins (eds) *Research as a Basis for Teaching*. London: Heinemann.

Swift, G. (1983) *Waterland*. London: Picador.

Sylvester, D. (1994) Change and continuity in history teaching, 1900–1993, in H. Bourdillon (ed.) *Teaching History*. London: Routledge for the Open University.

Tate, N. (1995) Speech to the Council of Europe conference on the role of history in the formation of national identity, York, 18 September.

Thompson, E.P. (1965) *The Making of the English Working Class*. Harmondsworth: Penguin.

Tobin, K., Butler Kahle, J. and Frazer, B.J. (1990) *Windows into Science Classrooms: Problems Associated with Higher Level Cognitive Learning*. London: Falmer.

Torrance, H. and Pryor, J. (2001) Developing formative assessment in the classroom: using action research to explore and modify theory, *British Educational Research Journal*, 27 (5): 615–31.

Unwin, R. (1981) *The Visual Dimension in the Study and Teaching of History*. London: The Historical Association.

Van Driel, J.H., Veal, W.R. and Janssen, F.J.J.M. (2001) Essay review of J. Gess-Newsome and N.B. Lederman (eds) (1999) *Examining Pedagogical Content Knowledge: The Construct and its implications for Science Education*, London: Kluwer Academic Publishers, *Teaching and Teacher Education*, 17: 979–86.

Verloop, N., Van Driel, J. and Meijer, P. (2001) Teacher knowledge and the knowledge base of teaching, *International Journal of Educational Research*, 35: 441–61.

Walsh, B. (1996) *History in Focus: GCSE Modern World History*. London: John Murray.

Walsh, B. (1998) Why Gerry likes history now: the power of the word processor, *Teaching History*, 93: 6–15.

Ward Schofield, J. (1993) Increasing the generalisability of qualitative research, in M. Hammersley (ed.) *Social Research: Philosophy, Politics and Practice*. London: Sage.

Watts, R. and Grosvenor, I. (1995) *Crossing the Key Stages of History: Effective History Teaching 5–16 and Beyond*. London: David Fulton.

White, J. (1994) The aims of school history, *Teaching History*, 74.

Wilson, M.D. (1985) *History for Pupils with Learning Difficulties*. London: Hodder and Stoughton.

Wilson, S.M. (1990) Mastodons, maps and Michigan: exploring uncharted territory while teaching elementary social studies. Paper presented at the annual meeting of the American Educational Research Association, Boston, 3 April.

Wilson, S.M. and Wineburg, S.S. (1988) Peering at history through different lenses: the role of disciplinary perspectives in teaching history, *Teachers College Record*, 89 (4): 525–41.

Wilson, S.M. and Wineburg, S.S. (1991) Models of wisdom in the teaching of history, *History Teacher*, 24 (4): 395–412.

Wineburg, S. (2001) *Historical Thinking and Other Unnatural Acts*. Philadelphia: Temple University Press.

Wineburg, S. and Wilson, S. (1991) Subject matter knowledge in the teaching of history, *Advances in Research in Teaching, Vol. 2*. Greenwich, C.T: JAI Press.

Wolcott, H. (1994) *Transforming Qualitative Data*. London: Sage.

Woods, P., Jeffrey, B., Troman, G. and Boyle, M. (1997). *Restructuring Schools, Reconstructing Teachers: Responding to Change in the Primary School*. Buckingham: Open University Press.

Wrenn, A. (2001) Build it in, don't bolt in on: history's opportunity to support critical citizenship, *Teaching History*, 96: 6–12.

Yin, R.K. (1994) *Case Study Research: Design and Methods*. London: Sage Publications.

Index